PRAISE FOR

The Anatomy of Seduction

Pastor Jack Hayford has always been such an inspiration to me. He was addressing lust and sexual integrity issues while others were denying they were huge issues in churches. The teaching in *Anatomy of Seduction* can help all of us avoid the temptations that can kill marriages and destroy souls.

STEPHEN ARTERBURN
AUTHOR, *EVERY MAN'S BATTLE*

There is nobody in the nation that has more wisdom, practical insight and spiritual sensitivity to the moral battles that men and women face in today's culture. Jack has not only proved to be a faithful shepherd living a life of purity and integrity but also has pastored thousands of men through his men's seminars and through the life of The Church On The Way. He has taught and counseled countless pastors and leaders and strengthened their moral fiber to live righteous lives in today's world.

I highly recommend *The Anatomy of Seduction* for all leaders and up-and-coming leaders. This is one book that you want to keep on hand.

FRANK DAMAZIO
PASTOR, CITY BIBLE CHURCH
PORTLAND, OREGON

Jack Hayford's riveting book *The Anatomy of Seduction* sheds light on individual and societal deceptions regarding purity, perversion and other sexual traps. Pastor Hayford not only uncovers the mechanics of seduction, but he also establishes a biblical plan for chaste living and deliverance from sexual sin.

MARILYN HICKEY
AUTHOR, *BREAKING GENERATIONAL CURSES*
PASTOR AND SPEAKER
FOUNDER AND PRESIDENT, MARILYN HICKEY MINISTRIES

With the authority of one who's been there, Pastor Jack Hayford highlights four simple, yet powerful, principles for finding freedom from sexual bondage. In addition, he presents biblical teaching on masturbation and oral and anal sex, subjects often avoided by the Church. *The Anatomy of Seduction* is an invaluable gift to all who seek complete freedom.

JOSH D. MCDOWELL
SPEAKER AND AUTHOR

Jesus taught us to pray, "Deliver us from the evil one." In *The Anatomy of Seduction*, Jack Hayford exposes the incredibly subtle wiles of the devil so clearly and personally that just reading the book will bring welcome, life-changing deliverance to many.

C. PETER WAGNER
AUTHOR, *CHANGING CHURCH*
CHANCELLOR, WAGNER LEADERSHIP INSTITUTE

The Anatomy of Seduction

JACK HAYFORD

Regal

From Gospel Light
Ventura, California, U.S.A.

PUBLISHED BY REGAL BOOKS
FROM GOSPEL LIGHT
VENTURA, CALIFORNIA, U.S.A.
Regal PRINTED IN THE U.S.A.

Regal Books is a ministry of Gospel Light, a Christian publisher dedicated to serving the local church. We believe God's vision for Gospel Light is to provide church leaders with biblical, user-friendly materials that will help them evangelize, disciple and minister to children, youth and families.

It is our prayer that this Regal book will help you discover biblical truth for your own life and help you meet the needs of others. May God richly bless you.

For a free catalog of resources from Regal Books/Gospel Light, please call your Christian supplier or contact us at 1-800-4-GOSPEL *or* www.regalbooks.com.

Cover design by David Griffing
Interior design by Stephen Hahn
Edited by Selimah Nemoy

Library of Congress Cataloging-in-Publication Data
Hayford, Jack W.
  The anatomy of seduction / Jack W. Hayford.
    p. cm.
  Includes bibliographical references.
  ISBN 0-8307-2969-0
  1. Sex—Religious aspects—Christianity. 2. Adultery. I. Title.
  BT708.H38 2004
  241'.66—dc22   2004013655

1 2 3 4 5 6 7 8 9 10 11 12 13 14 15 / 10 09 08 07 06 05 04

Rights for publishing this book in other languages are contracted by Gospel Light Worldwide, the international nonprofit ministry of Gospel Light. Gospel Light Worldwide also provides publishing and technical assistance to international publishers dedicated to producing Sunday School and Vacation Bible School curricula and books in the languages of the world. For additional information, visit www.gospellightworldwide.org; write to Gospel Light Worldwide, P.O. Box 3875, Ventura, CA 93006; or send an e-mail to info@gospellightworldwide.org.

DEDICATION

To the hosts of faithful shepherds serving the Bride of Christ, His Church, who, by their own sexual integrity, argue against the notion that the sad violations of trust so widely broadcast are normal. (Indeed, they are not.) And this book is written in the hope of helping reduce such instances all the more.

To the thousands of committed brothers I have pastored through the years, whose choice to follow Christ the Lord as growing disciples—with the same totality as they believe in Jesus the Savior—has included committing to love their wives in pure fidelity, while walking among all men with total integrity.

To the godly women I have pastored and served beside, whose lives have rejoiced my heart as I observed theirs—lives of holiness without snobbishness and purity without prudishness—extending an influence in raising, teaching or shaping the children within their care and igniting these children of light in this dark hour.

And to Anna, my precious wife and lover, and my devoted partner in ministry. Fifty years of living and growing together have only deepened my sense of the Kingdom nobility, the sweetness and the beauty that Father God saved for me and gave me when He arranged that I would meet and marry a Lady like you. How wonderfully He has kept us—always and only for one another.

CONTENTS

ACKNOWLEDGMENTS

It is with a distinct sense of gratitude that this book and its companion volume on sexual integrity, *Fatal Attractions*, come to the marketplace at such a time as this. These books were first conceived by Kyle Duncan, former publisher at Regal Books, and brought to fruition through the conviction and vision of Bill Greig III, president of Gospel Light Publications and Regal Books. Both men characterize the qualities that these books seek to engender and strengthen in today's discerning and dedicated disciples of our Lord Jesus Christ.

I am also indebted to Selimah Nemoy, editor of *Spectrum* magazine and of many of the other publications that flow from The King's College and Seminary, both in print as well as via other media. Her effective ministry includes providing seemingly endless resources for Christian leaders and readers at our Internet website: www.kingsseminary.edu. The incalculable diligence and patience she shows in distilling spoken messages to workable manuscripts make possible my delivering editorially suitable manuscripts to publishers in at least half the time, and probably with 100 percent more effectiveness.

And to our staff at the church and the seminary; to my assistant, Lana Duim; and to my wife, Anna, who is always so dependable a reader and helpful an analyst of my work—thanks to all.

Jack W. Hayford
Pastor, The Church On The Way
Chancellor, The King's College and Seminary

CHAPTER ONE

THE VELVET-LINED TRAP

Be sober, be vigilant; because your adversary the devil walks about like a roaring lion, seeking whom he may devour.

1 PETER 5:8

It was on a day over 50 years ago that an eight-year-old boy walked into the house of a friend for a morning of innocent play. While he did not realize it at the time—not for a minute—what happened that morning would, to some degree, become a decisive, though not defining, moment in his life. It decisively put into place an intrusive influence that he would recurrently face as he grew older, though not defining his destiny nor ruling the choices that he would make as year followed year.

I was that eight-year-old boy. Much of what follows in this book flows out of the struggle of forces that that intrusion characterized and that my decisions eventually neutralized—by the grace and power of God.

UNSUSPECTINGLY ENSNARED

My friend Don and I were sitting opposite one another in his living room, poring over a board game—probably Monopoly—and strategizing our next moves. We looked up when his teenage brother entered the room and sat down. He took out some pages from a folder that he was obviously hiding and furtively looked around—scanning the kitchen door where his and Don's mother was busy. Then quickly he handed us two pages and said, "Here, read this." He watched us with a smirk, exerting his teenage superiority and influence over us.

It was clear that we were being offered a secret—an inside track to something for "older boys." We both took the bait and began to read. The pages had been clipped from a book and described in lurid detail a crude, corrupt encounter between a man at a restaurant table and a waitress who had snuggled up beside him. Immediately, sexual exchanges began between them. While by today's standards the story would be relatively tame, it was nonetheless filthy, lewd and perverse.

Neither my eight-year-old mind nor my experience had any context for what I read, even though my basic awareness of the "birds and bees" of human sexuality was in place by this time. But youthful curiosity is powerful, and whispered hints of what really goes on between older boys and girls make a child a vulnerable target for almost anything that will even slightly increase his or her bank of information in this area. Both Don and I were incredibly ripe subjects for such a moment. Even now, I can remember it so clearly.

I was just a young child, but I still recall the way my heart rate increased to near explosion and how my head spun with the heat of the imaginary excitement. Yet what was being generated at both the emotional and physical dimensions wasn't the heat of a little boy who knew nothing of depth regarding

> Bondage may be deep or superficial, it may be fascinating or tormenting, but it is real.

human sexuality or sexual passion; it was the heat ignited by another source—the heat of hell.

I didn't laugh at the time—none of us did. Don's older brother revealed his smugness by virtue of superiority in years, but he was like most teenage boys of that time—with barely more knowledge than Don or I, and no more experience.

In the wake of those few moments, we all knew that we had been confronted with something new and—however filthy—intensely exciting to our youthful sensitivities. What I didn't know, and would not come to understand until years later, was that what took place in those brief moments that morning had registered a point of spiritual bondage in my life—a snare that would not be uncovered until three decades later.

SPRUNG FROM THE TRAP OF BONDAGE

I have never spent a dime on pornography. Yet well into my adult years, I kept finding myself engaged in a peculiar tug-of-war—one that always attempted to pull me in a direction I had firmly committed myself not to go. I never once gave in to that thing, yet my soul was repeatedly confronted with scuffles and skirmishes over it, much like being drawn against one's will into a wrestling match. I struggled with this problem as an adult, never realizing that a trap—one lined as if with the softness of velvet, seductive and sensuous—had been laid, and that it had snapped shut upon my innocent venturing and had ensnared a part of my soul.

Eventually, by the precious, discerning work of the Holy Spirit, I was led out—in one moment—through the labyrinthine ways of the mind in which (1) the memory of that morning was brought back to my consciousness, (2) I understood how infecting it had become, and (3) I saw how wonderfully Christ could spring the trap.

By using the term "ensnared," I want to be clear from the beginning about what must be acknowledged regarding the seductive potential of any violation of God's divine order for our human sexuality. At any level of exposure to the disobedient, the corrupt or the rebellious, not only are human mental, emotional and physical responses at work, but so also are *spiritual* forces, which the Bible calls "seducing spirits" (1 Tim. 4:1, *KJV*).

There is only one biblical word to describe the nature of such spiritual intrusiveness into the human life or personality: "bondage." It may be deep or superficial, it may be fascinating or tormenting, but it is real. And what I discovered was that, even as an innocent eight-year-old, I had been seduced—initiated into the corrupt by a cleverly devised plot of the merciless and fierce

Adversary of human souls. That Adversary manipulated the soul and the polluted mind of a writer of cheap pornography, and by his tawdry skill, eventuated the placement of the man's product into the hand of a teenage boy, and thereby subtly used that child's hand to plant such trash into the minds of two younger children. Thus, by the interplay of so many hands, a point of very real bondage was affixed into the soul of at least one child: mine.

The dimensions and impact of that moment would only become fully discerned and understood years later. Understanding and discernment are very much involved in my relaying the life-liberating and soul-defending principles we will study together.

Later I would learn how pornography is not only words or pictures but also a *spirit* motivated by a demon out of hell. I came to see principles that relate to all of us: how transactions often conducted unwittingly on our part (as well as consciously) lead nonetheless into a velvet-lined trap of seduction—a trap that is so smooth and deceitful, yet with such strength of grip, that it is seldom fully realized for the awesome power it wields over us until it begins to overtake and subvert so much that is good, righteous and life-giving in a well-intending person.

The story of how that happened to me is indicative of what happens to many people—often with tragic long-term consequences. A bend in the road at an impressionable age can turn the life of a precious young person far away from the future and hope that God promises His people in Jeremiah 29:11. The same story has had, for me, a glorious ending—not because evil was not the intended goal, but because the grace of God, joined to other godly influences in my life, brought a wonderful deliverance from the bondage that that childhood snare established and from the viciously intended plan that would otherwise have been the product of the snare's intrusion into my life.

IDENTIFYING THE DESTROYER

Hellish intrusion is always at hand. It is the relentless and calculated objective of a very real Being, and of the host of cohorts at his command, as our common Adversary makes his approach. He is ever and always merciless—his victims being targeted irrespective of age and without consideration for the rich and wonderful purposes of God for each human being.

Our Lord Jesus identifies our enemy, Satan, as a thief who comes to steal, kill and destroy (see John 10:10). Satan brutally seeks this objective at every point of human experience, existence and enterprise. He seeks to destroy domestically (ruining homes and marriages); economically (draining resources and bankrupting business pursuits); professionally (removing the prospects of fruitfulness and effectiveness in one's labors); physically (encumbering with affliction, sickness and death); and on and on.

Behind this Destroyer lies a trail of destruction as he works his wiles, brutalizing minds and emotions along the way and especially manipulating our vulnerability at that fundamental point of our identity—our sexuality. Once we have been seduced and snared at any point—and especially when we are caught in the velvet-lined trap of sexual bondage—the Enemy of our souls

- floods people with shame and guilt in order to *steal* their confidence and peace;
- deceives people into adopting habits that *kill* effective discipleship; and
- neutralizes believers' testimonies in order to *destroy* the life-transmitting power of their witness, their "ministry."

As I have elaborated with completeness and clarity in this book's companion, *Fatal Attractions,* the power of sexual sin and bondage is too profound for sexual sin to be considered "simply another kind of failure" or to be trivialized as "risky entertainment" or "just playing around."

HELD CAPTIVE BY THE CULTURE

I want to underline these realities for you, especially if you are a vibrant young person just coming into adulthood. You may be wondering why it's so important to defend yourself against the seducing influences of the world, when that means going against the rip-roaring tide of everything that is presented as desirable by the icons of popular culture. More than a generation ago, our society absorbed into its rhetoric the slogan, "If it feels good, do it," elevating the sensual over the spiritual, and enshrining covetousness and lust over wisdom and morality. Today, it barely takes watching network television, viewing a supposed-to-be family film, glancing at a magazine or tuning in to a three-minute MTV clip to be bombarded by the glamorization of immoral lifestyle choices and sexual images.

Learn it early, dear one: The agenda here is not hidden. The intended objective has become clear and unapologetic: to excite to sexual arousal (in the name of "informing" or "educating") and to entice to sexual indulgence (by suggesting that to be sexually disciplined is to be "inactive" and to be sexually indulgent is to be "active"). The result is the formation of a matrix of thought that reduces true humanity to something other than "persons" and that binds soul and body onward and downward toward the pit at the end of seduction's dead-end path.

This seduction may not involve a believer's consideration of an outright or blatant expression of sexual immorality. Rather, it may be the subtle deception that a select portion of the Enemy's tempting bait can be accessed without getting caught in his trap: lingering on the adult cable station while channel surfing, failing to be discriminating in the kinds of reading material permitted in the home, engaging in chatty flirtation over the Internet or entertaining one's sexual fantasies and imagination. It may be the temptation to compromise in subtle ways, having been deceived by the Adversary into valuating some sin as "not so bad" or not even as sin at all.

Or the seduction may be the blatantly inappropriate indulgences of fondling or French kissing a person who is not your spouse—practices that have gone from the restricted to the recreational. Today, we are witnessing at pervasive and disturbing dimensions (especially as it relates to teens and even preteens) the absorption of homosexuality, masturbation and oral sex into our culture, stamped with society's seal of approval. Tragically, this view has, at times, been validated by some in Christian circles.

CALLED TO BE HOLY

Yet if these seductions and deceptions were not detrimental to what Father God, our Creator, intended for our lives, He would not have provided in His Word warning after warning about sexual immorality, as well as the admonition that believers in Jesus Christ are to be holy—a way of living that is both *possible* and *rewarding*.

> Therefore gird up the loins of your mind, be sober, and rest your hope fully upon the grace that is to be brought to you at the revelation of Jesus Christ; as obedient children, not conforming yourselves to the former lusts, as in your ignorance; but as He who called you is holy, you also be holy in all your conduct, because it is written, "Be holy, for I am holy" (1 Pet. 1:13-16).

Holy living is not beyond our ability, because it is Christ in us who enables that holy living. Our ability to live holy lives is dependent only on the degree of our submission to Christ in us. Holy living is *desirable* because of the abundant harvest of spiritual fruit that such discipleship produces. Purity and self-control are among the foundational characteristics of believers in Jesus Christ who have genuinely given their lives to the Lord and who now live enabled and empowered by His Holy Spirit and not by their own inclinations (see Gal. 5:22-23).

For a number of believers, even those who walk in moral purity and those who enter purely into the covenant relationship of marriage, there come situations in which everything that's in us seems to be tested in the face of temptation. The Bible does not teach that we will never be tempted, but it does teach that we are fully equipped by the Word of God and the power of God to resist the temptation: "Therefore submit to God. Resist the devil and he will flee from you" (Jas. 4:7).

WISDOM OR HARLOT: CHOOSING BETWEEN TWO "WOMEN"

Keep your heart with all diligence, for out of it spring the issues of life.
PROVERBS 4:23

Seduction is the tactic of intentionally drawing us away from the purpose and will of God in our lives. While seduction is romanticized by our worldly culture, it is a powerful bait of the Adversary in his insatiable quest to steal the glorious fulfillment that God has designed and intended for us as His children.

One of the most telling portions of the Bible with regard to seduction is found in the book of Proverbs. In the opening chapters of Proverbs, two "women" are described: one is the personification of wisdom, and the other is the personification of sexual sin, depicted as a harlot and adulteress. While Proverbs also refers to this evil person in the male form (see 2:12), none of these passages is speaking more negatively (or positively) about either gender.

> # Seduction is a powerful bait of the Adversary in his insatiable quest to steal the glorious fulfillment that God has designed for His children.

Let me make it clear that women are neither more capable of wisdom than men nor are they more guilty of being seducers than men. Only human posturing of gender superiority—practiced by both men and women—breeds the unkind comparisons and destructive competitiveness that have prevailed and that still do in today's world. God never does that—He specializes in *people*—and He has created both genders with equal and glorious potential. So when uniqueness exists in either, it is for the betterment of the opposite gender, not for its dominance.

Thus, in this passage in Proverbs, the manifold blessings and benefits of a relationship with wisdom, which is depicted as a woman, are described:

When wisdom enters your heart, and knowledge is pleasant to your soul, discretion will preserve you;

THE VELVET-LINED TRAP 19

understanding will keep you. Happy is the man who finds wisdom (2:10-11; 3:13).

The other woman—the figure luring us away from wisdom—is described as "the immoral woman, . . . the seductress who flatters with her words" (Prov. 2:16). She clearly represents those things that entice us with false promises, drawing the soul away from the purity and perfection of God's intent for our lives. In the *King James Version*, this verse calls her "strange," in Hebrew *zuwr*, meaning foreign. She is not foreign in terms of ethnology; she is foreign to, *distant from and alien to*, God's created purposes for humankind's best interests. This "wisdom" is *apart from* the Lord, since she "forgets the covenant of her God" (v. 17). In other words, she no longer is of a mind-set ordered by the Creator's designs. And all of this is followed by the warning that to follow her leads to destruction: "For her house leads down to death, and her paths to the dead; none who go to her return, nor do they regain the paths of life" (vv. 18-19).

How many of us have, at one time or another, put God's wisdom on the back burner to embrace the world's so-called wisdom and found ourselves at a dead end? Nowhere in our lives is that more horribly damaging than when we have followed the seducer of our souls into sexual sin.

"Keep your heart with all diligence," the book of Proverbs (4:23) counsels. And immediately, in the three ensuing chapters, it gives recurring warnings against that flattery and seduction that beguile the soul into sexual sin (see 5:20; 6:24; 7:5,21). These warnings are repeated because the consequences of being seduced can be so severe: "As an ox goes to the slaughter, . . . as a bird hastens to the snare, [the individual] did not know *it would cost his life*" (7:22-23, emphasis added).

CREATED IN THE IMAGE OF GOD

For in the image of God He made man.
GENESIS 9:6

Fundamental always in discussing these themes is the issue of humankind's identity and purpose as designed by our Creator. With all the lures that modern society flings at human beings, our primary understanding of who we are intended to be is often mixed up, even for some believers. All humankind has been created in the image of God. That image—tarnished in fallen man— was restored through the death and resurrection of Jesus and is progressively being recovered in people who have welcomed Him into their lives. While the lust for many things is seducing— power, prestige and money being among the most potent—nothing more devastatingly corrupts God's high destiny for us at our most fundamental core of identity and purpose than yielding to sexual temptation or to the lure of indulgence.

As you begin this book, it's obvious that you are seeking to successfully navigate the minefield of temptation that today's culture spreads before all of us. You may be looking for help in discerning issues, addressing questions or defending against failure. It's possible that you are seeking answers to minister to precious people who have not yet surrendered their lives to Jesus Christ. Without receiving the gift of God's love through His Son, Jesus Christ, who is specifically called "the wisdom of God" (1 Cor. 1:24), none of us has a truly dynamic resource to counter the "wisdom" that the world argues in its program of deception. As believers, it is absolutely necessary to be equipped with God's strength in order to distinguish the deceptive ploys of the Enemy and to withstand them, and to receive the Holy Spirit's help in assisting or ministering to others trapped by them.

The starting place, of course, is to welcome Christ into our lives—to receive Him personally—because He is not only God's Wisdom but also the only Savior, God's gift from heaven to bring us home to the Father and into a life of fulfillment within His ways and wonderful purposes for us. If you are unsure about how you can receive God's gift of salvation in Jesus Christ, His Son, I have provided a guide to assist you in prayer—a way to honestly come to Him and begin life on His terms and in His love, today (see appendix 1). Let me urge you—before you go any further—to turn there and take the most important step that any of us could ever take: turning from our way and "wisdom" to Jesus, God's Savior and humankind's only hope for eternal wisdom.

Once we have received the gift of God's redemptive salvation through our Lord Jesus Christ, we are called to walk obediently and to advance within the joys and principles that unfold His ways for life at its fullest (see 1 Cor. 6:9-11; Col. 1:10). Becoming a true disciple—a sincere follower of Jesus Christ—will free you from any shallow mentality about salvation's goal. Too many people simply see salvation as a "quick dip" of God's paint roller, painting over the dirt to make them "nice and clean."

But two things must be kept in dynamic tension if we want to grow beyond spiritual infancy as followers of the Savior: First, God's great gift of salvation—the forgiveness of our sins—is real and worthy of our timeless and everlasting rejoicing. And when we enter this covenant of salvation by receiving the Savior, full acceptance in His love and forgiveness is a "given"—given to us in Jesus, once and for all. Second, however, God has *more* in mind for us than just forgiving our sins. He's very, very interested in growing up a family of sons and daughters who learn His ways, advance in them and lead others to do the same.

It is beyond our human capacity to realize the phenomenal

magnitude of what God is saying about us when He declares that He has made us *in His image*. The Lord has created human beings with a high destiny, and He wants us to learn how to relate to that destiny at greater dimensions than we may have previously understood. Through Jesus Christ, we are not only admitted into the Kingdom of God, but we also are destined to become its inheritors, as well as its agents here on Earth (see Matt. 25:34; Gal. 5:19-21).

DISCERNING THE TEMPTATION TRAP

Thus, it becomes incumbent upon us to discover how the Enemy's "agencies" seek to oppose and render ineffective our role as "agents" of Christ's Kingdom. Defending our hearts against those things that contaminate and corrupt is a matter of discipleship for believers in Jesus Christ. In my book *Living the Spirit-Formed Life,* I have sought to define the kind of life, experience and witness that is described in the book of Acts—the normal Christian life as conceived by our Lord Jesus Christ, which extends beyond the covering of our sins and assurance of eternity in heaven. The steps forward to the Holy Spirit-formed life are clearly set forth in God's Word:

1. Be *Spirit-born* by repenting for your sins and by putting your faith in Jesus Christ as your *Savior,* verifying the commitment by obeying Jesus Christ as *Lord* and being baptized in water (see Acts 2:38,39).
2. Be *Spirit-filled* by receiving the promise Jesus gave that His followers shall receive power—power to move in new dimensions of worship, praise, prayer, service and witness (see Acts 1:5-8; 2:1-4).
3. Be *Spirit-formed* by recognizing that the entry door of

new birth and the birthright blessing of Holy Spirit
fullness are only *beginnings*—both calling us as believers to *growth* in Christ's likeness and *discipleship* under
His lordship (see Rom. 12:1,2; Acts 2:42,46,47).[1]

Having lost the battle for our eternal souls, Satan's unre-
lenting program of thievery is to diminish discipleship and
Kingdom power among believers. To avoid becoming snared in
his velvet-lined trap, it is imperative that we believers learn how
to discern the bait of seduction and see beyond it. When our eyes
are only on ourselves, all human beings invite the tragic possi-
bilities of being "led away by various lusts, always learning and
never able to come to the knowledge of the truth" (2 Tim. 3:6-7).

However, as we move into this study—as we resolve questions
about the seductive nature of our present culture, especially its
warped sexual values (or absence of values altogether)—I am
specifically targeting the equipping of disciples like you with
help in this distinct and demanding arena of warfare. With eyes
fixed on God, and armed with His wisdom concerning how the
temptation trap is constructed, believers can be enabled and
empowered to be victorious overcomers against the deceitful
nature of the Enemy's enticements.

Discerning the temptation trap starts with understanding
the process by which this velvet-lined trap is laid in order to
seduce us away from purely worshiping Father God to placing
on the throne of our lives other gods—most notably, ourselves
(see Gal. 4:8). James 4:4 (*KJV*) puts it this way: "Ye adulterers and
adulteresses, know ye not that the friendship of the world is
enmity with God? whosoever therefore will be a friend of the
world is the enemy of God." Understanding this process by
which a believer's affections can be diverted from the Lord
begins with understanding the anatomy of adultery.

CHAPTER TWO

THE ANATOMY OF ADULTERY: THE GENESIS

The Setup for Seduction

You shall not commit adultery.

EXODUS 20:14

It is a testimony to God's goodness and grace, and unto His glory, that I can testify to and rejoice in the relationship that my wife, Anna, and I have. I am blessed to affirm my joy in the fact that I have been with only one woman in all my life—with only one woman in marriage and in a sexual relationship. We have just passed the 50-year milestone in our marriage, and we are pleased to be able to say that not only have we always and only been with one another but also we have never felt deprived. Rather, we have been overwhelmingly and completely blessed and enriched in *every* way.

It's certainly not as though neither of us has never faced temptation nor been unchallenged by the demands of growth in our mutual understanding or conflict resolution as we've grown closer and closer together through the years. But by God's great and sustaining grace, we have been preserved from those things that compromise the soul, erode the foundations of marital love and too easily become destructive—threatening to entrench in a marriage everything from dissatisfaction to disaffection and eventually dissolution and divorce. How grateful I am to be able to say that I do not have any memories to beg God to erase from my mind. Not only have I been faithful to Anna, but also I have never sat down and viewed a porn video or sought entertainment via the corrupting resources that surround and tempt us all today.

In describing these victories, I claim no personal glory to be able to affirm them. They have been won *only* by God's grace and have been sustained *only* by a dependency on the Holy Spirit's power. And acknowledging my dependence on God is an appropriate beginning to a very personal story I want to relate concerning a confrontation with myself, my weakness and, worst of all, the ferociously deceptive enterprise of our Adversary, the devil. What follows will make indelibly clear how un-self-righteous I feel when I testify to my fidelity to Anna and my constancy to sexual purity through the years. It will fortify your awareness of how truly grateful I am for God's keeping power and how fully conscious I am of the futility of any capacity to sustain sexual integrity in my life were it not for His grace.

Nearly Seduced into Failure

Allow me to share the story of the lessons I learned in facing the greatest challenge I have ever encountered in pursuing a triumphant life of sexual integrity. It concerns my near failure when, early in my ministry, the Adversary set a colossal, near-successful trap that first confused, then progressively deceived and finally nearly seduced me into the failure of my integrity, my marriage, my family and my ministry. Let me share transparently

> The Adversary's devices are never predictable in their approach, though they are always certain in their objective.

with you an incident in which I came frighteningly close to adultery, opening up within these pages as I have with tens of thousands of men and ministers over the years, hoping that my testimony—and the lessons learned amid the fires of warfare for my soul—will help others realize victory themselves.

This incident took place many years ago, before we came to our pastorate in Van Nuys, California, where the visitation of God's power brought about The Church On The Way. At the time, I was employed at the headquarters of my denomination, where I was engaged for nearly 10 years prior to pastoring The Church On The Way. There I worked beside a host of devoted, dedicated believers who were all committed to serving Christ with zeal and pure dedication. The struggle against my soul's integrity did not take place in an environment in which one would expect to become vulnerable to sexual entrapment. However, the Adversary's devices are never predictable in their approach, though they are always certain in their objective.

One more thing as I begin the account: I want to emphasize that my near failure was not a setup occasioned by any insensitivity or unavailability to me on my wife's part. It was not derived from any unhappiness or deficiency in our marriage. In short, I wasn't deprived of a fulfilling life at any point of our union, and I wasn't on the prowl—looking for kicks, flirting around or playing games. These facts are not stated to justify myself, though I do want to protect my wife and verify that she contributed nothing to my weakness. I rehearse them because they underscore how hideously deceptive and cruelly clever satanic devices may become, even under the best, purest or finest of circumstances. And also they evidence how totally vulnerable a human heart and sensible mind can become to deception and destruction, even when everything around would argue that a believer's disciplines and purity of motive in Christ's service would render him or her secure from either the flesh or the devil's success against moral integrity.

HIS WILL IS OUR COMMAND

And the world is passing away, and the lust of it; but he who does the will of God abides forever.
1 JOHN 2:17

Let me begin by establishing the authority of God's Word on the subject of adultery and His will for our lives. We live in a culture that increasingly trivializes human peccadilloes. There are even those in Church circles who at times shrug off the severity of sexual indulgences in the name of "grace." Therefore, we need to start from the foundation of how God views marital infidelity.

There is no ambiguity present, rather only absolute clarity and unmistakable demands, as God's Word addresses the subject of complete, unbroken and total sexual integrity within marriage. In Exodus 20:14, the seventh of the Ten Commandments is "You shall not commit adultery." If nothing else in the Bible referenced the matter at all, sexual fidelity is obviously a settled matter by this one reference. All humankind are called to this point of accountability.

However, the subject is made a further issue where Christian discipline is concerned, where the expectations of a believer in Jesus are stipulated in absolute terms. First Thessalonians 4:3-4 is but one of many references in which the New Testament reinforces statements of God's will. This passage states that all who have been redeemed through Jesus Christ should "abstain from sexual immorality; that each of you should know how to possess his own vessel in sanctification and honor."

With this, it has always seemed both desirable and important not only that we agree regarding the authority of God's Word but also that we be reminded that His commandments are not given as burdens but as *livable and fulfillingly liberating* directives. They are boundaries given to bless, mandates issued to bring richer meaning to all of our lives and living. As Proverbs 7:2 refreshingly puts it: "Keep my commands and *live*" (emphasis added). All of God's commandments—given to Israel upon their deliverance from generations of slavery and bondage—were and are intended to set His people *free*. They have not been imposed upon us to make our lives an unpleasant drudgery of laborious religiousness. Nor have they been randomly given to pinch life into a shriveled wad of mechanical responses that reduce our humanity and remove the sheer joy, the *joie de vivre*, that our Creator has always intended us to know. God's commandments are given out of love, and they are not impossible to keep, which is evidenced by His Word's own commentary on the matter—words that affirm not only the *blessing* of His commands but also the *promise* of enablement for our living in obedience to them:

> For this is the love of God, that we keep His commandments. And His commandments are not burdensome. For whatever is born of God overcomes the world. And this is the victory that has overcome the world—our faith. Who is he who overcomes the world, but he who believes that Jesus is the Son of God? (1 John 5:3-5).

Thus we see how beautifully His commandments are given to ensure our living successfully and with fulfillment; indeed, we have a "hope of glory" (Col. 1:27) that is not only eternal but also present as a temporal dynamic that will bring fullness and freedom to each of us who lets Jesus Christ have the reins of our lives.

So in addressing the subtlety of seduction and the intoxicating power of sexual deception, first, I am affirming the sobriety and absolute nature of the issue, and second, I am asserting the worthiness and the total desirability of obedience to God's commandments above any degree of surrender to sin that deception may suggest. We *can* defeat the flesh and the devil! This is an account that not only describes an agonizingly miserable self-discovery of the weakness of my own flesh, but it also relates the awesomely mighty supremacy of Jesus Christ when His power to resist and to overcome is invoked by even the weakest disciple.

A VERY PERSONAL STORY

Let me invite you on a journey; one that integrates a very personal story with a number of lessons that have been learned
through the combination of trauma and triumph that the
episode eventually brought about in my understanding. I ask for
your patience as you follow along, because I've learned from
experience that in telling this, it is most effective if the lessons
are integrated into the story's telling. But to relieve any appre-
hension you may have, let me give the ending here at the beginning: (1) God kept me from adultery; (2) He called me to risk
telling the story; and (3) the principles the story illustrates and
brings to light have become a means of deliverance and trans-
formation for the multitudes I've told it to. So, let me begin.

Following Anna's and my first pastorate, when we planted a
new church in Indiana, I worked for nearly 10 years at the headquarters of our denomination. A large number of people were
employed there, and among them was a woman with whom I
often worked on committees and special projects. It was in that
environment that the slow process of seductive deception was
set into motion.

Mutually focused with other team members on projects—
and ironically in this case, on evangelism—this woman and I
were both enthusiastic about the same thing. People working
together will often feel an affinity toward one another. Yet over
a period of five months, a gradual confusion began to set in. The
vast majority of that time was spent simply in the enjoyment of
working with someone who—while not attempting to in anywise
be seductive herself—was harmonious to be around; she was a
person of equal spiritual commitment to reaching the lost and
was as excited as I was about the project we were working on
together. It was in this apparently insulated and harmless, spiritually focused and well-intended atmosphere of pursuing a God-

honoring mission that slowly, but relentlessly, the lust of the flesh and the conspiracy of hell worked in tandem to bring an emotional entrapment.

This entrapment did not happen all at once. It began in an atmosphere of innocence during months of working together, and then it crystallized into a confusion that seemed to fog focus and later to explode emotions in a very short period of time. It is strategic to understanding, if one would avoid such a trap, to know that—at least in my case—the actual time involved, once our conversations became inclined toward more personal thoughts and feelings unrelated to the work project, was only a short span of a few weeks. This contrasted with the previous months of innocent partnership in labor, during which neither of us realized the craftiness of the Adversary's designs nor the vulnerability of our humanness.

We—two Christians, neither of us bent toward the unworthy and neither with any prior habit or practice of carnal indulgence, flirtation or compromise—were being *set up*. (Again, I mention this not to dignify myself or the woman but to underscore how the best and purest intention or background is no guarantee of security from the Enemy's devices.) Gradually, I began to recognize that something was slipping. An erosion of the singularity of our focus on the project was taking place, and I became aware of romanticized thoughts that would occur in my own mind (and be fought back—but only temporarily). Today, I would recognize that velvet trap—a trap that evidenced in mildly adjusted attitudes and in peculiar turns of conversation that should have been taken as warning signals—but I didn't then. I did not realize that the Adversary was progressively exploiting both our innocence and our unawareness to subtly lay a land mine that was designed to destroy more lives than I even care to attempt to enumerate.

WISDOM IN TIMING A TESTIMONY

Allow me to interject something here, as a point of reference to any person who has ever come close to, or actually participated in, the sin of adultery. While this event took place several decades ago, it was 10 years before I spoke about it or made reference to it in any public setting. This was so for a number of significant reasons: First, I did not want to do anything to reawaken the emotional pain that I had caused my wife. It would be wise for everyone reading this to consider that if there has ever been any episode in the past that may have been a strain or struggle in your own marriage relationship, especially where there has been some intrusion by a third person, once the situation has been clarified and dealt with, both you and your spouse would do well to be silent on the subject for a minimum of two to three years. Healing cannot take place in wounded people who keep picking scabs, reopening wounds and bleeding over the problem again and again. Pain needs to be brought to the Cross and left there.

Second, I did not discuss this publicly for a long time because I needed to distance by years the possibility that the other person's identity could be guessed. She is as equally a devoted servant of Jesus Christ as I am, and there was no intent whatsoever on our part to develop an infatuated relationship that moved close to the edge of an adulterous one. Neither of us was looking for the chance to have an affair or to be unfaithful to what we knew to be the call of God and of Jesus Christ on our lives. (In fact, her future moved forward in purity as well, with a happy marriage protected from intrusion or violation, and with the blessings of a fulfilled family.)

Third, I wanted to avoid personal presumption. I waited 10 years before talking about it because I did not want to presume too quickly that I had learned how to prevent the possibility of adulterous entrapment. And as I relate this story now, I want to say that I *still do not* presume to *ever* have mastered this subject, and I will always refuse to claim any righteousness on my own part. To this day I walk in humility, not only remembering my near failure, but also ever mindful of my absolute need of Jesus' life, grace and power in my life, for only the Holy Spirit can fully keep any one of us when we are fully available to be kept. Any person who falls for the vain supposition that he or she is beyond the possibility of seduction immediately becomes all the more vulnerable to it.

So it is that I contextualize my cautions as well as my purpose in sharing this very personal story. The thousands I've shared it with, both publicly and privately through the years, have attested to the practical value of the wisdom that can be discerned and distilled from it. It is a means to forewarn and to forearm men and women equally, to stop in their tracks all who will listen, to turn them away, if they are tempted, from even vaguely considering a flirtation, embracing an infatuation or pursuing any trail that can become a pathway of sexual impurity. My willingness to be transparent regarding one of the most difficult times in my own life—indeed, to risk someone's thinking me less than a sincere servant of my Savior at any time of my life in Christ—is a price I long ago chose to pay. It is a risk I believe to be worth it, if my story enlightens, enables or equips any believer either with insight against their own flesh's capacity to be deceived or with discernment against our common Enemy's will to destroy us.

I want to dismantle the anatomy of seduction and to open eyes and hearts to discern adultery's stylized temptation. The Adversary has a custom-made assault for each person's deception. Yet even though the variety of our circumstances and personalities is great, the basics of our human nature, as well as the components of *both* sound-minded clarity and deceived, confused thinking, have a common denominator. So let's move ahead as we sort these out and learn the pathway of discernment unto obedience.

THE LOOK OF LUST

You have heard that it was said to those of old, "You shall not commit adultery." But I say to you that whoever looks at a woman to lust for her has already committed adultery with her in his heart.

MATTHEW 5:27-28

Contrary to the supposition that adultery is solely a physical sexual act, the Word of God is unambiguous concerning the fact that adultery is far more and far deeper an investment of our beings than that. Adultery begins with, and is essentially an engagement of, the *eyes*, the *heart* and the *mind*.

The words of Jesus in Matthew 5:28 speak with severity regarding any careless or indulgent glancing—and even more, fixating our eyes upon something: "Whoever looks at a woman to lust for her has *already committed adultery with her in his heart*" (emphasis added). Lust is not something that springs from a moment's glance. Lust is something that happens out of studied gazing, mental preoccupation or flirtatious, exploratory or repeatedly returned glances. It comes as a result of *studying a subject:* looking at a person and allowing a growing, eventually consuming, attraction to him or her to develop. Of course, to look at a person and then turn one's eyes and refuse the temptation to become mentally preoccupied doesn't mean adultery has been committed. What Jesus is addressing is not merely temptation that surrounds us by proposition or by opportunity at first nod;

He is addressing the *entertainment* of that thing in the mind or the soul. According to Christ, adultery takes place when there is studied analysis—when the machinery of the mind and emotions begins producing imaginations and attitudes that compromise personhood, cheapen relationship and indulge the thought life in sexual fantasy.

The sadness of what I share with you here is that there are so few in our society who would even think that this is an important issue. Far from being prudes, we who are disciples of Jesus Christ are people who live beyond the foolishness of this world. The common expression once routinely heard, "the wisdom of the world," has little to stand on today, since there is hardly a residue of anything in the world as we know it that might be called wisdom on any subject of moral or spiritual consequence. We are surrounded by a society either so consumed with its own quest for privatized, self-seeking advancement or so dissipated physically or morally by endless pleasure seeking, that relatively few people think much about true values or about taking life seriously.

This is not to say that such superficiality is calculated. To the contrary, it is simply the product of a blinded culture, numbed to the preciousness and value of the Creator's high purpose for each person's being. The Bible describes the sad departure of humankind when separated by sin from the fountainhead of life in a relationship with God:

The whole world lies under the sway of the wicked one (1 John 5:19).

[The gospel] is veiled to those who are perishing, whose minds the god of this age has blinded, who do not believe (2 Cor. 4:3-4).

You once walked according to the course of this world, according to the prince of the power of the air, the spirit who now works in the sons of disobedience (Eph. 2:2).

To note the worldling's insensitivity to God or His ways is neither to accuse nor to condemn; Jesus said He didn't come to do that. The purpose is to observe that we will never be able to take from the world our signals regarding *most* of life's primary values, including the matter of how we live as sexual beings. Clearly, believers in Jesus Christ are called to live *outside* the folly of the world and *in* the wisdom of God.

In examining how deceitfully the Adversary uses seduction to draw us away from God's purpose for our lives, Jesus Himself extends the definition of adultery beyond the act of marital unfaithfulness and into something that takes place in the human heart. In addition, our definition of adultery must be broadened beyond those who are married. None of us—whether single or married—may pretend that we are not in an environment that necessitates our vigilant exercise of caution, discernment and wisdom.

THE HAND OF HARM

If your right eye causes you to sin, pluck it out and cast it from you; for it is more profitable for you that one of your members perish, than for your whole body to be cast into hell. And if your right hand causes you to sin, cut it off and cast it from you; for it is more profitable for you that one of your members perish, than for your whole body to be cast into hell.

MATTHEW 5:29-30

Not only does the Bible say that adultery is an engagement of the eyes, the heart and the mind, but it also says that adultery involves the *hands*. Why would Jesus have mentioned the hand, having only earlier mentioned the eyes, which lead to the thought processes? Irrespective of some pop-Christian opinions to the opposite, it is obvious that our Lord, in the most tasteful way, is dealing with any number of misuses of our hands—spanning the spectrum of sexual compromise. Outside of marriage, the list would include everything from groping to impure manual sexual stimulation, from fondling to masturbation.

Christ's life in us *can*, and *will*, make purity desirable — and possible.

It is no accident that Jesus bonds the eye's indulgence to the hand's actions and indicates that the heart that entertains adultery is violating God's order for sexuality. His drastic words cannot be overlooked or taken lightly. When Jesus says to tear out your eye or to tear off your hand, obviously He is *not* proposing that a believer amputate or gouge out a body part. But He *is* pressing an issue that calls us to a violent confrontation with temptation's summons to self-gratification. Our surrender to the lordship of Jesus Christ involves the movement of our whole being, under the guidance and by the empowerment of His Spirit dwelling in us, into the realm of His Kingdom's rule, to govern our eyes and hands as well as to fill our hearts and minds.

And consistent with His Kingdom's good news, not only is there forgiveness for all that we haven't been, but also His life in us *can*, and *will*, make purity desirable—and possible.

THE HEART OF UNFAITHFULNESS

As I have noted previously, in my own situation the process of seduction took place slowly and subtly. The Adversary's mode of operations is, in progressive stages, to craftily deceive people. Having an understanding of his stealth, along with wielding the weapon of wisdom (see Eph. 6:17), will arm believers who truly desire to avoid the temptation trap and enable them to walk as people who are healthy, holy, liberated and fruitful in Jesus Christ.

Further, I believe that these principles apply in *every* regard to *every* pathway of sexual disobedience. While I am describing and defining adultery here in a way that includes its essential meaning—sexual involvement with a person who is not your spouse—as well as its broadened biblical meaning, I want to expand that definition to apply also to anything that would either

- command a believer's vision in a way that is contradictory to their role as a disciple of Jesus Christ or
- occupy a believer's mind or body in a manner that yields to sexual lust, un-Christlike behavior or carnal indulgence.

This is not taking liberties with God's Word, but holding our feet to the fire of truth as it is revealed through all of the Bible. When God's people compromised their heart's commitment to Him in *any* way, drawing them away from their fidelity to His ways, the voice of the prophets called it adultery (see Jer. 13:27; Ezek. 23:37; Hos. 7:1-4). Laced through Bible history, these episodes, in which God's covenant people drifted from their love and commitment to Him, illustrate how the seepage of society's relativistic mind-set and the increased prevalence of sexual permissiveness can pollute worship, corrupt commitment, fracture faith and destroy discipleship. In situation after situation, beginning with the fall of humankind in Genesis, through Israel's repeated failure and rebellion and finally to the total seduction of society by the Great Harlot in the book of Revelation, the Bible tells us of disastrous cases in which people lost their moral distinctives because they chose their own ways over God's (for example, see Ezra 9).

As the Lord's people, we are warned time and again not to allow the spirit of the world to contaminate the integrity of the new life we've been given in Christ, not to bite on the tasty bait that the Enemy dangles before us as a part of his seduction program.

If the first-century Church wasn't immune to the assaults that called for confrontation on this theme and needed to be warned against the essential dangers inherent in violated sexual integrity, we have every reason to be warned in our day as well. The apostle John's words draw strong lines for us to heed:

> For all that is in the world—the lust of the flesh, the lust of the eyes, and the pride of life—is not of the Father but is of the world. And the world is passing away, and the lust of it; but he who does the will of God abides forever (1 John 2:16-17).

CHAPTER THREE

THE ANATOMY OF ADULTERY: THE REVELATION

The Stages and Stealth of Seduction

Blinded by the fog of confusion and well-crafted stylizings of Satan, I completely missed discerning anything of a progression of deception—the alluring, seductive tactics of the Adversary's manipulation of the reality that I was shaping and the evil that was dogging my way. But when God's grace brought the explosion of light that burst upon my soul and occasioned the mighty deliverance that ensued—thankfully, before sexual compromise had occurred—I was able to see it. In the aftermath, I examined the folly of the path that had seemed so innocent at first and, later, so disgusting to my soul. Over time, while outlining the lessons drawn from this near catastrophe, I discerned four stages of seduction, which I now arrange in four downward steps: *opportunity, exploration, deception* and *bondage.*

FIRST COMES OPPORTUNITY

I think the doorway of opportunity for sexual seduction and possible failure will open to every person at some time or another. Nothing so basic to our life and our responses, to our longings and our potential fulfillment within God's order, will go without a challenge by the dark lord of hell. Our sexuality is not only a precious life-begetting gift; it also holds a wonderful life-enriching quality within the divinely prescribed circle of marriage's delights. Believe me, Satan is too hateful an adversary to not seek to pollute and destroy this fountainhead of possible fulfillment. Moreover, the potential sensual ecstasy related to our sexuality makes it a point of essential discipline, lest it dominate us rather than our ruling and protecting our own personhood according to God's order and wisdom. Couple these facts with the stark realities of the way everything in our culture today argues for the justification of not only taking but also pursuing every manner of sexual indulgence. Even so, as I've said, my vulnerability was not the result of surrendering to the world's mind-set; I was not seeking an affair, nor at the outset was any such possibility in view. If it had been, I would have fled it. But the opportunity existed in the regular occasions of simply working together—and, amazingly, working on a project intended to bring people to Jesus Christ!

Neither I nor the woman I worked with was attempting to be cute, coy or suggestive in our manner toward one another. Yet I realized later that at the root of the attraction that developed between us was the relational opportunity our recurrent occasions of working together provided. We weren't in a private place; we were in an open office with others nearby. But as months of intermittent but frequent contact took place, I began to be ensnared by the simple fact that she evidenced more than simple respect: There was a show of mild admiration toward me—enough for either my human pride or insecurity to feed on. From the earliest sense of possible impropriety in this relationship, that was all that took place until the day our conversation came to the moment I call the breakthrough of evil.

This was not a moment of physical contact; it was not an exchange of cheap suggestiveness nor plans made for a rendezvous. Rather, evil broke through before any of the obvious manifestations that anyone would immediately recognize. The Adversary of our souls is too cunning to post a signboard summoning rebellious acts of corruption, but quietly, almost inconspicuously to our perception, he drops calling cards incorporating seduction's suggestions. They seem innocent or trivial at first, but as I discovered afterward, evil lurks in these progressive steps of an advancing seduction.

Step 1: Mental Preoccupation About the Other Person

Mental preoccupation in itself should be sufficient warning, yet we human beings have a tremendous capacity to deceive ourselves and to tolerate the supposition that "he/she is just a friendly person and is so nice to me." It's not necessarily a preoccupation with the physical attributes of a person's body. If I had been thinking lewd thoughts about this woman all that time—which I wasn't—I would have long before been forewarned. She was just increasingly "on my mind." *Beware of mental preoccupations.*

Step 2: An Unusual Desire to Be Near or Around the Person

At times when committee meetings were called that did not require her presence, I gradually found myself suggesting she be there because it seemed "practical," given her place helping me. Though I didn't actually calculate it at the time, this afforded even more reason for us to engage in conversations after meetings. *Warning*: Mental preoccupation breeds the quest to "just be around" the other person—enlarging the base for opportunity. (This may manifest itself in other ways: for example, looking for the opportunity to go just slightly out of your way to be near the person; positioning yourself in a roomful of people to gravitate toward an inevitable contact. Such actions are essentially born of the flesh, but once given place—and I've warned people of this many times—Satan will get involved, and you'll find him manipulating contact opportunities that the flesh can easily delude itself to see as God's providence, rather than the Adversary's plots.)

Step 3: A Growing Desire to Give Frequent Compliments

One of the rules that I have learned is to not give *personal* compliments to women other than my wife and daughters. There is a difference in commending a person's good work or their diligence to duty, affirming their worth or value as a person, and in noting, "You look especially pretty today," or "That dress is particularly attractive," or "I can't imagine getting along without you." Today, society has a whole set of approved verbal come-ons that essentially announce the intention of an improper relationship—come-ons such as, "I find myself very attracted to you." Even the simplest word set can become a personal vent for desire—desire yet unrecognized for where it can lead you. (Let me say, there *is* a fitting time for expressing gratitude to persons with whom you work, just as Anna and I take occasion together to express special appreciation to the ladies—and, of course, the men as well—who are part of my office staff.)

I want to stress that what happened in my life took place in the context of people who were *seeking mutual objectives as members of a team dedicated to serving the Church of Jesus Christ.* This is a critical point of vulnerability, especially for those who serve in Christian ministries or in any similar environment in which people in crisis are being helped. The opportunity for deception, such as I experienced, can also arise when a person is called to console others who are struggling with deep problems, heartbreak, disappointment or any of the other painful or troubling things that beset many. It is a very real possibility that in the quest to comfort—thereby being with the other person regularly—mutual emotional confusion can capture the soul of even the most devoted servant of Jesus Christ, especially when ministering to the opposite sex. This can also happen when this servant attempts to affirm people who feel rejected or neglected and, in seeking to reinforce the person's sense of worth, ends in becoming unduly preoccupied with comforting that person (or rewarded by the person's gratitude to the point that their own comfort becomes a quest). Deception in such an environment is too commonly a setup for seduction, and it must be neither ignored nor denied.

Step 4: The Supposition That an "Innocent" Fling or Flirtation Can Be Indulged

It is a self-deception—a ruse of the flesh—to suppose that any one of us can make a temporary decision to throw off restraint, or inhibition, and get away with it. The marketing lie "Whatever happens in Las Vegas stays there" illustrates the vain idea that any one of us can say, "Just for a minute [or a seemingly allowable brief moment] I'm gonna let myself go." Not only is there no escape from moral responsibility for the believer in Christ, but also the possibility that the Adversary will capture that moment of exposure in order to secure a beachhead of evil in a soul or a relationship is too great to risk. In Luke 21:19, Jesus admonishes, "By your patience possess your souls." It's His directive *never* to "just let go"; it's His call to "get a grip" and keep it!

In this verse, the Greek word for "patience" (*hupomone*) means to bear up under pressure. That is the call of the hour as the pressures of the seducing spirits linked to the last days are loose and at work (see 1 Tim. 4:1). Also in Luke 21, Jesus prophesies concerning the increasing intensity of evil, and His words, "possess your souls" (v. 19), are a pointed call to *retain dominion* over our minds and our emotions. It is His call to self-control in these extreme days when so much is out of control.

AFTER OPPORTUNITY COMES EXPLORATION

"Opportunity" refers to the entry levels of seduction. The next stage, exploration, manifests as preoccupation when a person seeks, in time and as occasion presents itself, to discover *whether feelings are mutual*. In other words, the antennas are raised, wondering if the other person thinks or feels the same. It is a conscious quest for feedback.

It is never my desire to appear to give Satan too much credit for anything, and it is certainly not my habit to overlook the enormous contribution the flesh—our human will, self-seeking, carnal motivation, prideful indulgence, etc.—can bring to any situation. However, I am not reticent to address the spiritual reality that brings inspiration and enablement to evil pursuits, just as surely as the Holy Spirit brings the same to godly pursuits.

In the exploration stage, one opens the door to that arena where demonic intrusion finds entrance. And peculiarly, "amazing coincidences" occur that can convince a person that there is something so right—maybe even God's will—to what is going on in his or her mind and feelings about this relationship. For me, what had begun as mutual interest in a task occasioned eventual expressions of amazement at the affinity that we supposed evidenced something unique between us: "I was just thinking that same thing!" For some people, it can be that as the two are talking together, both say exactly the same words at the same time, and they laugh at their apparent "being so much alike." But such a moment of laughter indicates more than just what may be humorous; it introduces a certain mutual delight—a sense of internal gratification that argues to one or both of them, *"It's true. We really* are *in sync in a special way."* What begins as simple similarity and grows to an observed affinity progresses toward a disintegration, since, where deception is at work, there is no goal of uniting *anything*—only of dismantling God's purpose for people and of breaking hearts, homes and hopes.

Though it is a regretful, embarrassing thing to remember now—a memory that stirs both disgust with myself and anger at my blindness to the Adversary's conspiracies—I remember how, when working on the assigned project, I would intentionally stroll over to the woman's office and we would interact, ostensibly about the project. In doing so, it was common that our ideas were exactly the same about the project, and my mind would wander to a second possibility: *If we thought the same about it, might she feel the same feelings I did?* She was on my mind so much that I started to wonder if maybe I was on her mind, too. So, occasional hints seemed tolerable, hints like how we were both interested in the same things. Smiles were exchanged over how unusual a mutuality we had on "so many things" and, worse, over the idea that that mutuality might possibly signal something of beauty or significance, something that required definition and thereby discussion: "We think so much alike, and we certainly make quite a team when they give us a job to do, don't we?" And we began to sense that warm feeling that happens when there comes such agreement.

Exploration of the idea that our "brother-and-sister relationship in Christ" was "especially close" was an attempt to spiritualize what was increasingly a deception that progressed with both of us. I emphasize here that there was nothing of physical involvement, but the frightening specter of a relationship on the edge and en route to going over the edge was gradually taking shape.

Our supposing that we were just talking about our work was evidence that our hearts had already begun to be stolen from under Christ's lordship and were being (though unacknowledged by either of us) compromised from the commitment that each of us had to our God-given partners. The *married* man I was (and thankfully, still am) had now been seduced—not by a woman, but by my own deceived heart—having succumbed to an undetected, adulterous mind-set. An adulterous mind-set neither requires physical interaction nor mental imaginations of intercourse (neither of which was involved here); rather, it involves the violation of two kinds of commitment: *godly commitment to personal integrity* and *spiritual commitment of heart and soul to our spouse, which is intended by the vows of marriage.*

The fog of confusion blurred my clear vision of God's Word and blinded me to the meaning in God's Word of the godly man's call to be "the husband of one wife" (1 Tim. 3:2). The spirit of that text not only disallows polygamy but also confronts the fragmentation of a heart—a place to be reserved solely for your spouse—by the emotions that occur when another person is allowed in. In other words, the Bible addresses more than simply a person's marital *status* in the eyes of social law; it addresses an individual's present marital *commitment* in the eyes of God.

This becomes very practical in our mind-set regarding marriage. A solid view of this principle could head off any number of the Adversary's efforts at distracting and distorting. For example, suppose that during a week when things aren't going too

Excursions of the mind — explored, tolerated and imaginatively toyed with — are neither more nor less than adultery.

smoothly at home, a married person takes occasion to entertain thoughts about how it would be if he or she were married to someone else—someone who is more appreciative, patient, understanding, sensitive, intelligent, reasonable, etc. Consider the guy whose mind trips back to some girl who was a college flame or the guy who wonders if he might have been better off marrying so-and-so.

It may seem a brutal application of the words "the husband of one wife," but by honest definition, such excursions of the mind—explored, tolerated and imaginatively toyed with—are neither more nor less than adultery. Though physical adultery isn't involved in the mental concessions just described, taking Jesus' teaching that what involves the mind can ultimately be as destructive as what involves the body (see Matt. 5:28), "adultery" is an appropriate description nevertheless. In the same manner, the apostle Paul's words to Timothy are not being exaggerated when seen in the light of a man's (or woman's) call to live as the husband of one wife (or the wife of one husband).

The embarrassing truth is that in the midst of a horribly disgusting self-discovery, I learned how duplicitous evil is when it seduces the mind to believe in the impossible proposition, *I think I'm in love with two people.* I want to explore that thought later in this chapter, as a part of describing the two most deceptive thoughts I experienced; but for now I want to put a biblical reality on the table in front of us: The flesh needs to be brutally confronted at times. Dear one, you and I will give far less place for the devil's successful intrusion into our lives when our flesh is taken far more seriously and is dealt with with a matching severity (see 1 Cor. 9:27; Eph. 4:27).

FINALLY COMES DECEPTION THAT LEADS TO BONDAGE

Deception and bondage go hand in hand. One flows into the other. When this occurs, blindness has *taken hold*—not blindness to what is wrong but blindness to the *reality* of the compromise that has occurred. This is an activity of seducing, or deceiving, spirits, which the Bible describes: "Now the Spirit expressly says that in latter times some will depart from the faith, giving heed to deceiving spirits and doctrines of demons" (1 Tim. 4:1).

Deceptive Spirits

Perhaps no more profound a word can be employed to describe the seduction that the spirit of this world accomplishes than *planos,* the Greek word translated as "deceiving" in this text and the word from which we derive our English word "planet." The ancient Greeks used this word for the same astronomical entities we call planets, but they were actually calling those bright orbs deceivers. Why? In ancient times, the navigators of the vessels that plied the broad expanses of the oceans learned that it was impossible to make a sighting on one of those "stars" to be certain of where they were. They, of course, didn't know that those "stars" in actuality were planets, which revolved around the sun, nor did they know the vast difference in the distances between Earth and the stars and planets. However, these sailors came to realize that they could, with reliability, sight in on most stars to accurately determine their location and thereby sail the right course to their destination. And they also learned that the "deceivers" (*planoi*)—the moving stars—would only lead them to confusion or destruction if they tried to determine their position by them.

It isn't difficult to see why the Holy Spirit stirred the apostle Paul to use this word to warn us about the demonic enterprises of these last days. We dare not take our directions from the "no such thing as absolute truth" relativism of our culture's attitudes toward almost everything, including sexual values. In addition, we would be wise to see the profound analogy between the erratic movement of a dead, non-light-producing planet and the deceiving spirits of this world. The Bible says that Satan "transforms himself into an angel of light" (2 Cor. 11:14), and of these spirits, it says, "There is no light in them" (Isa. 8:20). And Jesus said, "If one walks in the night, he stumbles, because the light is not in him" (John 11:10). So the word "planos" refers to demons that seduce—like planets—giving off a display of false light and beauty but leading to destruction. The same is true of the work of seductive spirits: to give improper relationships the deceptive appearance that they are star-spangled and glorious. That's the way seduction happens.

False Comparisons

As the deception of seduction took over in my life, I found myself recurrently tempted to compare this woman with my wife, Anna. Again, I reiterate that my dismal story was never brought about by anything of neglect or inattentiveness toward me by my dear wife. But let me add: Even if I *had* been, in my view, neglected, it would have been no excuse for my behavior! Let the lie be put to rest: The verbal oath of marriage and the bonds that God declares the oath places upon our commitments cannot ever be argued away.

Thus, the growing mental entrapment of my mind—my flesh being seduced by the skills of a lying spirit—progressed to the point that I began making comparisons, though obviously not *sexual* comparisons since nothing sexual ever took place. Further, they were not comparisons regarding appearance, for my wife was an attractive, appealing woman (and one who, after 50 years of marriage, still looks as beautiful to me as ever!). But the Deceiver struck at whatever point of penetration he could make, inviting me to compare by *noting the differences* between Anna and me in ways of relating and ways of thinking, in attitudes and styles, and the *similarities* that this woman and I had in these same areas.

The mental process that was going on in my mind violated two values: (1) It was captivated by the ways that the other person was like me (a not very subtle concession to *self-love*); and (2) It failed to put value on one of the most blessed gifts God offers all of us in our marriage unions: a spouse who, by their *difference* from us, provides a balancing and complementing addition to our lives (not a reflection of ourselves, but a refreshing "other" who brings dimension to the marriage and life that we have together).

The success of such seduction is that, given time, the gift of the partner God has given us seems decreasingly interesting and not as fascinating as the rising "star" (the planos) that is drawing us off course and toward disaster. And the astounding thing about deception is that once it gains a foothold, it has a way of increasing itself exponentially. Dissatisfaction, discontent, irritation and other evidences of displeasure with anything other than "my way" all seem to argue for the rightness of the course being pursued.

Verbalized Thoughts

The verbal amplifications of the deception, manifest in my earlier mentioned excursions of conversation seeking to give some righteous or worthy definition to the relationship, finally permitted the evil to break through. Comments such as "We really have an unusual relationship, don't we? What are we supposed to mean to each other anyway?" were not really questions. They were explorations of a deepening quest to receive affirmation of something that neither of us had the right to offer the other.

Today, remembering that verbal tripe, I want to scream aloud to anyone so duped, "Get real!" If you do have a "special" brother or sister in Christ, I can assure you that he or she won't be any more sexually or emotionally attractive to you than your biological brother or sister! You don't seek the constant approval, touch or time of your sibling, nor do you go out of your way to be with him or her; so don't do it with your brother or sister in Christ!

Such ideas, which I now recall with frustration and irritation over the memory, were just glossing a deception. The deceptive thoughts tried to give credibility to the relationship with a line of reasoning that was spawned in hell, twisting my mind's perspective to a place where I was on the brink of self-destruction, though I thought it was the height of insight via a unique sensitivity to "someone special." With the verbal interaction between this woman and me, the lie began to deepen and take root. That brought the bondage. For me, this happened without my realizing how deep it really went.

THE TWO MOST DECEPTIVE THOUGHTS

It is a point of real embarrassment for me to reveal the two most horrible ideas to which my mind was finally led before the Lord delivered me. Yet I have shared this testimony over the years at meetings and gatherings, and do so now in print, to audiences from many different backgrounds, types of ministry service and age groups, because I deeply desire that no one else would ever experience surrender to such deceit.

As I said at the beginning of this chapter, God, by His mercy and grace, spared me from actually committing sexual immorality, which would have been the absolute worst thing that could have taken place. We never came close to arranging that possibility, yet prior to my deliverance from bondage two hideous deceptions entered my mind.

The first of the two deceptions was my seduction into presuming I genuinely loved two women. There were times when a hint of this entered the conversation: "It's such a mystery that we feel such deep affection toward one another and that, even so, I don't love Anna any less." She would affirm her respect for Anna, and I have no doubt that she was sincere. She was not a vixen out on the make. We were two people trying to do right but actually doing terrible wrong, without realizing how deep the bondage was becoming.

After the Lord delivered me, I realized that thinking I could love two women was nothing less than adultery. When, in

Jeremiah 3:8, the Lord said that Israel was an adulteress, it was because they imagined they could love both the Lord God and other gods as well. This surrender to adultery—God's people absorbing pagan practices while being deceived into thinking they were still serving Him—is at the root of so much failure and loss even today.

Further, when we look at New Testament disciplines and mandates for godly behavior, it is irrefutable that there is no such thing for anyone in the Lord as a husband with two wives. Let me be absolutely clear: *Anytime a married man gets the notion that he has the ability to love two women, he has, in no uncertain terms, enthroned himself as a false god.* When it comes to the kind of marital affection that commands real devotion, romantic attention and wholehearted care, if a third person ever becomes involved, then the toxic sludge of deception has penetrated all the way through.

The final word on it: Sir, if you so much as *think* you can love two women, you're an adulterer. And the same is true if you are a woman who thinks she can truly love two men. (And in this book, it should be unnecessary to say that the same holds true if the other person involved is of the same gender.)

The second horrible thought that entered my mind was the sinister question *What if something happened to Anna?* There were times when I was so deceived that I would wonder, *This is such a special relationship. Why would God put this relationship in my life unless He had some plan for it?* Though I am ashamed to say it, the response that would dance in and out of the background of my mind (I did not permit this thought to take shape fully in the front of my mind) was *It's not right to think this way, but I wonder if something's going to happen to Anna. Is there perhaps an accident that's about to take place? Maybe with this relationship God is preparing me for my future.*

THE DAY OF DELIVERANCE

When finally the Holy Spirit smote my heart and brought His revelation and conviction, I was shocked to realize that so foul a spirit had succeeded in seducing me to wonder whether God was preparing me for the future by bringing this woman into my life. And, oh, how I wept! Obviously not because I would ever have sought or wished my wife's death, but because my soul had become so entranced by deception that my mind would even entertain the concept!

> Healing takes time, and that time must be given to love's nurturing and patient care.

When by His mercy and grace the Lord brought me to the place of confession, renunciation, repentance and deliverance, it was a painful, hard, emotional time for both Anna and me. I had vandalized my wife's emotions. She had not known what I had been thinking until it was over, but that did not mitigate the tremendous emotional trauma I caused her by making my precious wife feel rejected.

Anna was exceedingly gracious, exceedingly righteous in her response, but that doesn't mean it was any less hurtful to her. It also does not mean that I was any less guilty. Adultery—even the emotional brand I was entrapped in—is not something that can be whitewashed in a moment. It required many, many months for emotional healing to take place, and something on the order

of two years for a full-dimensioned restoration of peace, security and mutual confidence in our marriage. This was absolutely
not because of Anna's unwillingness, but simply because the
most forgiving soul still is a human one, and healing from a violation of any kind—just as from a terrible accident—takes time.
That time needs to be honored, and it must be given to love's
nurturing and patient care.

In the decades since, Anna and I have often shared this
story with groups of couples, each telling it from our own perspective, in order to help them discern the anatomy of seduction and adultery. After we tell them what happened, then
we sit before them and let them ask us questions about the
aftermath. I believe that the transparency of our testimony
has imparted encouragement and enlightenment (and perhaps, in some cases, conviction) to others, strengthening their
commitment to fidelity to Jesus and to their marriage. But
believe me, even though enormous grace and goodness from
God have far surpassed my embarrassment over the near success of the Adversary and the shameful show of my fleshly
weakness, surrendering to seduction is *not* worth it. This is not
a story to relive—it is a warning to receive and a seductive path
to reject.

DEFENDING YOUR HEART FOR GOD

Though my story is told from a male perspective, the application
of truth gleaned from it can be made by both men and women.
I write to you, brothers and sisters who are committed to Christ
but who, like me, live in a body of flesh in a world that is hell-
bound.

The Word of God is rich with wisdom, and the gift of the
Holy Spirit is abundant with discernment if we will but open our

eyes, our minds and our hearts to receive it, refusing to allow ourselves to be deceived and seduced. As we seek to grow in that discernment and wisdom and to defend our souls from the inevitably heartbreaking consequences of adultery, there are five laws of life that I believe are imperative for every believing man of God to follow. These laws ought also to give pause to any woman who senses a man acting in this manner toward her, thus offering a glimpse of the velvet-lined trap.

1. Don't be alone with any woman except your wife.

This law does not need to become a legalistic imperative, but it ought to be observed as a general rule in every married man's life in order to prevent offering territory to the Enemy of our souls.

2. Don't indulge an attraction by giving compliments.

As I've already shared, the web of enticement that compliments weave can easily become a net of bondage. There is propriety in affirmation, but there is equal impropriety in seeking to gain a place of notice from another person or in giving place to a surge of unworthy attraction under the guise of being nice.

3. Don't accept a protective role toward a woman other than your wife.

There's a discernable difference between assuming a protective role and being in a leadership position that requires you to watch over your subordinates. What I am talking about here falls into the realm of *falsely affirming your sense of identity and your masculine ego* by taking care of, or watching out for, another woman. As a Christian, it's your job to be gracious toward *all people* in the spirit of God's love. But your care, in the deeper sense discussed here, only belongs to the one whom God has given to you and you alone.

4. Do tell a strong, trustworthy brother in the Lord what you're dealing with.

The Word of God in Proverbs 27:17 declares, "As iron sharpens iron, so a man sharpens the countenance of his friend." Secrecy and isolation are among Satan's most powerful tools. Be honest about any temptation you are going through by confiding in a strong, trustworthy brother who will partner and pray with you—*not one who will validate what's wrong,* but one who will exhort and encourage you to do what is right.

5. Do pray in the Spirit and cover any potential situation with the Blood of Jesus Christ daily.

The Holy Spirit will reveal any root cause for confusion, and the Blood of Jesus Christ will bring deliverance, liberty and protection. Spiritual warfare is waged by praying in the Spirit (see Eph. 6:18), and the same Holy Spirit of intercession will enable you to pray *beyond* the limits of even your best discernment. I sometimes call the Holy Spirit the Great Psychiatrist—just as we call Jesus the Great Physician—because He has the ability to bring into the light those things we don't really perceive about ourselves. Praying in the Spirit has a way of bringing perspective to our understanding and exposing underlying issues that have opened the way for bondage. As we acknowledge those issues, He uses our confession and renunciation of them, as a person might use a sword, to cut the cords, or chains, that have held us captive.

This liberating power flows through the Cross of Christ and is ministered by the power of His Blood, which the Bible says will disintegrate both the power of sin's record against us and its grip upon us, and will abolish the capacity of the powers of darkness to sustain control over us.

He has made [you] alive together with Him, having forgiven you all trespasses, having wiped out the handwriting of requirements that was against us, which was contrary to us. And He has taken it out of the way, having nailed it to the cross. Having disarmed principalities and powers, He made a public spectacle of them, triumphing over them in it (Col. 2:13-15).

Let me urge you, if you are facing any dimension of the deception or bondage I've described in this chapter or elsewhere in this book: Go to Jesus in prayer! Call on the Holy Spirit to flood you with His grace. Invoke the authority of Jesus' Name, and welcome the cleansing, delivering power of His Blood. As a wonderful old hymn says:

'Tis the grandest theme through the ages rung;
'Tis the grandest theme for a mortal tongue;
'Tis the grandest theme that the world e'er sung,
"Our God is able to deliver thee."[1]

CHAPTER FOUR

BEHIND CLOSED DOORS

Let no one say when he is tempted, "I am tempted by God"; for God cannot be tempted by evil, nor does He Himself tempt anyone. But each one is tempted when he is drawn away by his own desires and enticed.

JAMES 1:13-14

Understanding the anatomy of adultery, as well as the stages and stealth of seduction, provides us with a map that helps us to navigate the minefield of temptation's traps. The Holy Spirit will underscore these warning signals when we find ourselves faced with the decision of whether to serve God or self—especially in regard to the morality of practices and habits cultivated "behind closed doors." When confronted by those challenges, the choices we make in our moral and devotional lives are what define us either as disciplined disciples of Jesus Christ or simply as believers in Him.

Let me share with you the story of one brother who sought to make the right decision.

Jeff brought the book with him and set it on the table, though it hadn't been much of a comfort or validation for the problem he faced. We met for an early morning breakfast at a coffee shop near my office and sat in a corner booth, away from where anyone else could hear our conversation. Jeff is a dear, young brother who genuinely loves the Lord, and the book was written by a Christian author who proposed that masturbation ought to be viewed as an acceptable point of adjustment for a believer's life until marriage.

"When I first read this book, Pastor Jack," Jeff began, "I felt liberated. But then all the confused feelings I had came back." He went on to talk about the condemnation and guilt he'd felt about his habit of masturbation. He'd hoped that by offering himself a solo sexual release, it would preserve his virginity for what he looked forward to being a happy Christian marriage later on. But Jeff's sense of violating God's will for his life persisted, even given the compassionate (though spiritually misguided) permission to continue his indulgence.

While I understood this author's attempt to be sensitive to the pain and frustration of people who are habitually drawn to masturbation, the idea that it is acceptable—simply because sincere people labor with sexual tension and need the "release"—is as ludicrous as saying that *any* physical expression is justified by the excuse "That's how I feel." The source of this contradiction is an age-old, ongoing battle between two diametrically opposed forces: spirit and flesh.

HEAVYWEIGHT CONTENDERS: SPIRIT VERSUS FLESH

Walk in the Spirit, and you shall not fulfill the lust of the flesh. For the flesh lusts against the Spirit, and the Spirit against the flesh; and these are contrary to one another.

GALATIANS 5:16-17

Among the questions posed by believers who seek biblical and moral guidance with regard to their sexuality, I am often asked, by both single and married Christians, about practices that include masturbation and oral and anal sex. I want to address the subject of masturbation in this chapter; further counsel may be found in appendix 4. To begin our discussion, we first need to look at what the Word of God says about the struggle of human beings' *carnal mindedness* versus the biblical summons to us as disciples of the Lord Jesus Christ to walk in the Spirit and to live under His control with His assisting power.

Although Scripture assures us, as believers, that there is "now no condemnation to those who are in Christ Jesus" (Rom. 8:1), this assurance is followed by the prerequisite that we "do not walk according to the flesh, but according to the Spirit" (v. 1). This verse is not speaking of people who *persist* in sin, but of those who stumble and who, by the exercise of confession, repentance and renunciation, then move away from it. As believers in Jesus Christ, we have the privilege of walking without condemnation because we are promised that "if we confess our sins, He is faithful and just to forgive us our sins and to cleanse us from all unrighteousness" (1 John 1:9).

The essence of the Lord's summons to holiness has to do with a believer's *commitment* to a direction in life; it's about continually moving forward in the Lord's way. When we are walking "according to the Spirit"—though at times we may stumble and fall into some type of sin (not necessarily sexual)—our eyes, hearts and minds will still be fixed on a spiritual goal.

Our spirits undergo a life-or-death struggle against the flesh. Underscoring this struggle, the Bible describes the carnal mind as being antagonistic and hostile to God:

> For to be carnally minded is death, but to be spiritually minded is life and peace. Because the carnal mind is enmity against God; for it is not subject to the law of God, nor indeed can be (Rom. 8:6-7).

In fact, the carnal mind is *always* at odds with God.

In this passage the Bible is not talking about Satan or demons; rather, it's talking about the human mind that is *given over* to the conviction that flesh ought to have its own way. The entrance of such a mentality into the mind-sets of some believers within the Church today (often through books like the one Jeff read) causes these people to justify attitudes that corrode conviction and that are dishonest about the meaning of discipleship. In some cases, scriptural prohibitions are written off as passé and out of touch with contemporary society. This tendency to trivialize sin, or the flesh, is essentially a concession legitimizing a believer's submission to un-Christlike expressions of the Adamic nature—the nature of fallen man.

I want to be very clear: I am not against people who are trapped by habits of masturbation. Neither am I suggesting that masturbation is a satanically inspired activity or something that will, in itself, damn a soul or separate a believer from God's love. Rather, I want to assert that masturbation is a *carnal* issue—one involving the human mind and will—and that any submission to carnality is opposed to the best interests of any of us who are committed to following Jesus, the Lord. Seductions surfacing from the carnal mind—whether they involve the lust for sex, money, prestige or power—may not destroy the soul, but they most assuredly will hinder our growth toward true maturity and spiritual effectiveness.

There is joy, fulfillment and fruitfulness beyond all that we can imagine in serving the Lord. Living a life that is filled and formed by the Holy Spirit in us surpasses any temporal pleasure

> Living a life that is filled and formed by the Holy Spirit in us surpasses any temporal pleasure that surrendering to seduction may provide.

that surrendering to seduction may provide. As we have already seen, it is by living *by God's laws* and *in His ways* that we may truly—and most fully—enjoy His gift of life to us.

THE SEDUCTION OF SOLO SEX

Helpful to our understanding, especially in a society that is constantly redefining its values by twisting the meaning of words, it is revealing to discover the actual derivation of the word "masturbation." This word comes from the Latin *masterbari*, which is defined as "virile member+*turbi* disturbance" in the Oxford Dictionary, the most complete dictionary of the English language. In discussing the word itself, this dictionary explores the history of the word and notes the possibility that it came from the words *manis* (for "hand") and *stuprum* (for "defilement"). In other words, the most authoritative dictionary in the English language demonstrates the likely derivation of the word "masturbation" as defilement by use of the hand and concludes with the direct definition "To practice self-abuse."[1] (The general definition in virtually all sources is to manipulate one's own genitals or those of another for sexual gratification.)

Now, for the sake of avoiding confusion, let me also make clear what activities I am *not* including in this definition. *I am not referring to nocturnal emission* ("wet dream"), which is the natural release of pent-up semen that occurs in men generally as the result of a dream of sexual fantasy. Some have argued that masturbation is nothing more than a dreamed fantasy, but there is a radical difference between involuntarily ejaculating during a dream—which is an uncalculated subconscious fantasy of the dreamer—and consciously setting one's mind to think sexual thoughts and then using one's own hand to release the semen that is produced.

I am not referring to mutually agreed lovemaking practice within marriage. I have been asked by couples if there is anything in Scripture that might indicate it is improper for them to stimulate one another's genitals to orgasm in foreplay, for example, or during the wife's menstrual period or in the late season of pregnancy when she is not capable of intercourse. My answer to them is that I see absolutely nothing wrong in that regard as long as it does not become a substitute for their normal expression of their sexual communication in the future.

I am not referring to an infant's self-discovery. Parents need to respond thoughtfully to the little child in the bathtub who's just beginning to discover and handle their genitals. If a parent reacts with either shock or indifference, long-term problems can ensue. It's a challenge to every parent to plan in advance how to address such an eventuality in a simple and natural way. In any case, this is not masturbation.

There is one other thing that I am not referring to, and with this point, I realize I tread on sensitive ground because I don't want it to seem at any time as if I am granting license or suggesting a casual attitude regarding this matter. But I do believe there's a vast difference between an adult's calculated habit of masturbation and a *frustrated teenager's impassioned self-indulgence that is followed by guilt.* I do not at all mean that I believe teenage masturbation is a good idea. Neither do I believe that masturbation ought to be excused as simply a ritual of growing up. But if I'm talking to a serious-minded Christian young person who finds himself or herself in a struggle or inner conflict over masturbation, I always seek to show patience and differentiate isolated occasions of failing to achieve self-discipline from studied, self-justifying habitual indulgence, practiced especially by a grown or married person.

RELEASE OR REJECTION?

Now after you have known God, or rather are known by God,
how is it that you turn again to the weak and beggarly elements, to
which you desire again to be in bondage?
GALATIANS 4:9

The book Jeff showed me—and other books like it—proposed that masturbation is nothing more than a necessary, biological release. Yet for believers in Jesus Christ, the issue is whether I am foremost a *biological* being, whose physical nature dictates my response to what the Word of God teaches, or a *spiritual* being, who has the capacity to receive the fullness of God's Spirit and to progressively move away from the carnal mindedness of the world that provokes indulgence of my flesh.

And in that regard, when we talk about solo sex, are we really talking about release? Or are we more accurately talking about *rejection*—the rejection of our commitment to the Word of God, to the disciplines of a believing walk and to the wholeness of God's intended purpose, destiny and fulfillment for our lives?

In defining those seductions that take place "behind closed doors," I urge every believer in Christ who is genuinely interested in growing as a disciple of the Savior to see how surrender to the practice, or habit, of masturbation essentially rejects the self-discipline that refuses carnal indulgence of the mind, body or spirit. Consider these three:

- *The surrender to sensuality*—submitting to the flesh, to one's body's desires
- *The surrender to fantasy*—submitting to soulish emotions and lewd imaginations that compromise the heart
- *The surrender to deception*—pretending that none of these things makes any difference

Such surrender, eventuating in deception, leads those who do so to allow their minds and intellects to become shaped by the casual stance of the world's mind-set, a mind-set that endorses casual sexual immorality and perversion as normal. Succumbing to fantasy and willingly giving one's mind to its wanderings and lusts are a refusal to take Jesus' words regarding the "thought" of adultery seriously (see Matt. 5:28).

In contrast, the Bible calls us, as Jesus' disciples, to operate as ones who "have the mind of Christ" (1 Cor. 2:16)—a biblical command that confronts the practice of masturbation. The number of Christian writers and counselors who refuse this

instruction from God are neither taking the command seriously nor regarding the spiritual implications inherent in masturbation. Again, the practice—while neither separating a soul
from saving grace nor denying the believer's *intent* to grow as a
disciple—is nonetheless counterproductive to one's spiritual,
emotional and mental maturity. What is legally tolerable for a
believer and what is pragmatically and spiritually advantageous
are two different things: "All things are lawful for me, but not
all things are helpful; all things are lawful for me, but not all
things edify" (1 Cor. 10:23).

Yet on a widespread level, masturbation has become
approved as *morally innocent* and *spiritually immaterial*. In such a
philosophical and increasingly amoral climate, I cannot too
strongly urge that we confront this stepping-stone to confusion
for the unworthy escape clause it is becoming to many—an
escape *from* self-discipline *into* a moral fog that can only eventu-
ate in further compromise—usually pornographic pursuits.

CONFRONTING THE CULTURE

Christian leaders need to be honest with the facts. We dare not
yield to a *cultural* notion and thereby allow such misguided
thinking to become peppered throughout the Body of Christ.
Wherever that potentially polluting trend seeps in, I urge a
forthright consideration of three assertions opposing the place
of solo sex in the life of a disciple of Jesus Christ.

**1. Masturbation, as culturally accepted today, is world-minded
and leads toward sin and personal bondage.**

Jeff's book said that masturbation was merely the act of making
love to the one we love the most. Glaring at us from the outset,
that definition touches at the heart of the matter: the self-

centered, indulgent nature of our culture that worships self as god. What Scripture calls us to is neither self-hate nor the nega-tion of our sexual capacities but rather *devotion* to Jesus Christ: "You shall love the LORD your God with all your heart, with all your soul, and with all your mind" (Matt. 22:37).

Our love for Christ will dictate an obedience to the disci-plines of *His lordship in our lives*—an obedience that the Holy Spirit will help us walk in. That flow of Spirit-led living will bring about the maximum release of every happiness and contentment that God intended for us to have, including our sexuality.

2. Any attitude or practice that inclines toward or accepts the cultural standard of masturbation as a Christian norm has adopted a world-minded orientation on the subject.
However noble it sounds, the proposition that solo sex is a legit-imate means to retain one's virginity is faulty and without merit. In my years of counseling people, I've found that people who practiced masturbation prior to marriage were *more likely* to violate the biblical standard on premarital intercourse because they'd formed a habit of indulging in sexual release when tempted.

What is at issue isn't whether Christians masturbate but rather, since Christians do, whether we should standardize solo sex as acceptable Christian behavior. To agree to that would clearly be to accept the world's mind-set—a proposition that is opposed in Scripture:

> I beseech you therefore, brethren, by the mercies of God, that you present your *bodies* a living sacrifice, holy, acceptable to God, which is your reasonable service. And *do not be conformed to this world*, but be transformed by the

renewing of your mind, that you may prove what is that
good and acceptable and perfect will of God (Rom. 12:1-
2, emphasis added).

God's Word is direct in its cautioning us about accepting the
world's mind-set. Adopting that mind-set is a trend that, once
allowed to gain momentum in the soul, will inevitably bring
tragic results for the believer: "For if, after they have escaped the
pollutions of the world through the knowledge of the Lord and
Savior Jesus Christ, they are again entangled in them and overcome, the latter end is worse for them than the beginning"
(2 Pet. 2:20). This argument is not to engage in fear or guilt tactics but rather simply to affirm that the subtle snares of the
Adversary are craftily set and cunningly camouflaged by the
world's way of thinking.

3. Masturbation is selfishly indulgent and potentially dangerous.

I have often been asked if the sin of Onan was masturbation: No,
it was simply selfishness, but it resulted in his death. Let me
relate the account from the Bible and then clarify my point.

In Genesis 38:8-10, we are introduced to Onan. His brother
Er had died, leaving Onan obligated to fulfill the ancient custom
of fathering a child to secure his brother's inheritance. The
assigned practice was for the living brother to "go in to" (v. 8), or
have intercourse with, his brother's widow and impregnate her.
The child would belong to her, not as a son to the natural father,
but as a substitute son for the dead father, thus guaranteeing the
family's future maintenance of their property rights under the
laws of the land. There were, of course, sexual implications to this
custom, but its main purpose was economic: to provide a means
for a man's inheritance and property to pass on to his family.

When his brother Er died, Onan was expected to fulfill this obligation in order to produce an heir. The Bible says that Onan did accept the privilege of having intercourse with his sister-in-law; instead of impregnating her, however, he removed himself before he ejaculated, his semen falling on the ground. The Bible's description of God's judgment for Onan's action is more than blunt—it is sobering and confrontational.

Yet the issue was not with the fallen seed but rather with the failure to serve the moral responsibility of providing an heir for his brother's house. God's anger at Onan was not for masturbation—that's not what Onan did—nor was it for the simple fact of interrupted copulation. It was for his selfishness: (1) for accepting the enjoyment of a sexual encounter without genuine concern for the responsibility it carried with it and (2) for refusing to bring a child into the world, knowing that the child (while not reducing Onan's own intended inheritance) would disallow his capitalizing on the larger inheritance he would have if his brother had no heir.

Let us not miss God's point, because otherwise the judgment will seem unduly hard. In the culture of that time, a woman with no husband or male child was a person destined for poverty and its inherent bondages. Onan's action was not nearly as bad as his attitude: His action was brutal, but it was born of deadly selfishness, a deadliness the Bible underlines with the manifest judgment of God's punctuating the point.

Thus, while the sin of Onan has no direct application to masturbation, it does contain a message regarding the potential danger present in self-consuming solo sex. The message is not that masturbation is verifiably dangerous to one's mental or physical health but rather that the fantasizing that invariably accompanies it can easily lead to endless illusions and preoccupation with mere orgasmic fulfillment (i.e., the quest for "kicks" without the responsibility of relating to people as persons). The emotional immaturity that is nurtured via masturbation is a ready pathway to merely viewing people as objects to be used rather than as persons to be valued. This is especially true when masturbation is accompanied by pornography, as is so often the case. And it is not inconceivable that repeated indulgence in solo sex can lead to a separation from reality that later plays to brutality. Even if that brutality were never to become physically abusive, I've found it to be hurtful in marriages: for example, when a spouse deprives his or her partner of the true interactive joy of genuine, mutual self-giving, having formed solo-sex habits of thought and practice and the attitude that "my satisfaction is all that's important."

Masturbation *is* dangerous, but certainly not because of the old wives' tales of giving people warts or making them go blind. Those ridiculous propositions never were the case and in their peculiar, folksy way simply added fuel to the very carnal tendency to trivialize masturbation as a compromise of, first, true maturity and, second, commitment to self-discipline.

The real danger behind the acceptance of solo sex as normal (if not desirable) for a "release" is in the way in which it reflects the growing attitude among many Christians: one that is unwilling to confront the requirements of the Cross in the believer's life and the cost of self-denial as a discipline for godly living. These concessions open Christians to the spirit of the world, and once that door is opened, ever-deepening levels of bondage easily ensue. Such bondage, which is yet to be discussed in detail in chapter 5, is the grip that results from having voluntarily stepped into a trap, over and over again, all the while thinking, *It's simply a release.*

AVOIDING CONDEMNATION—
ACCEPTING DISCIPLINE

"Is masturbation forgivable?" you may ask. The answer is yes. The affirmation of this allows me to further emphasize that *nothing* in these pages is designed to breed condemnation, to set myself up as a self-righteous critic or to resource a band of legalists like the Pharisees, who were more desirous of damning people for sexual failure than of delivering them from its guilt and bondage, as Jesus did. *All* sexual sins are forgivable, but the fact that sin may be forgiven should never make it a matter of casual concern.

Jeff was worried about whether my disapproval of solo sex made him unacceptable to me. My heart went out to him and I responded (and if necessary, *you* hear me, too). "Jeff, I will never withhold my acceptance of *anybody* who fails in *any* way." Wherever and whenever a sincere heart seeks an understanding one, I believe we, as believers in Jesus, are always obligated to reveal the loving heart of God to that person, irrespective of how broken, how confused, how tormented or how weak he or she may be. Jesus says, "All that the Father gives Me will come to Me, and the one who comes to Me I will by no means cast out" (John 6:37). We are all sinners in need of the Savior, and our acceptance of each other should be based on those terms.

However, *acceptance of a person* should not be equated with *approval of sin* or with the supposition that sin doesn't make any difference. This distinction—between acceptance and approval—has become blurred of late, both in our culture and in the Church. While the Bible does not say, "Thou shalt not masturbate," we believers, who are called to be disciples, are to "lay aside every weight, and the sin which so easily ensnares us" (Heb. 12:1). Jesus Christ calls us as His own and calls us to refuse the deadweight of fleshly indulgence as well as the sin-binding ways of the world-spirit.

Thus, in the spirit of Christ's purpose and call for our lives, we are here examining the contrast between two voices: first, *our Savior's* call to practical purity and holiness of life as His disciples, and second, *our society's* call to self-indulgence, especially in regard to how we address our sexual desires, drives, identity and involvements.

CONFIRMING OUR COMMITMENT

In concluding the matter of answering the host of questions I've had people ask me about masturbation and the objections raised by those who have suggested that it should be regarded more casually, I offer two more practical facts, which I have distilled from seeking the light of God's Word and inquiring of other leaders who are equally committed to growing as disciples of Jesus Christ.

1. Solo sex violates an internal witness.

Let me emphasize that as a rule I have not been the one who brings up the subject of masturbation in counseling sessions. People do! And I hasten to say that I have never had even one occasion among the many counselees I have ministered to (believers and nonbelievers alike!) who did not acknowledge an inner sense that masturbation was at least questionable, if not fundamentally wrong. However, I must acknowledge that pastors and counselors have told me that, due to the increasing paganization of our culture, this is decreasingly the case because a culturewide searing of moral conscientiousness is taking effect. Nevertheless, the truth is that believers in Christ, once reborn by the Holy Spirit, are called to a "renewing of the mind" (see Rom. 12:1-2), and in the newness of that renewal, virtually all intuitively question or reject solo sex.

This is only explainable by accepting the obvious reality that God has built a monitor into the human psyche that says, *This is not what you've been constructed to do.* That's why, despite the Christian endorsement for solo sex that Jeff read in a book, he knew in his heart that it wasn't right. Accordingly, how important it is that we do not run down the rabbit trails of philosophized self-indulgence but instead give God, and not our flesh, the benefit of any doubts. If unbelievers are held accountable to *conscience* regarding their relationship to God, even if they don't know the Bible (see Rom. 1:20-21), how much more ought we to heed the Holy Spirit's call to stop performing "dead works to serve the living God" (Heb. 9:14)?

Although masturbation is not directly named as a sin, the inner witness of the Spirit will speak to the soul concerning its being *in the spirit of* clearly named sins. For example, among the expressions of sin cataloged in Romans 1:18-31 (and notably, sins committed in direct defiance of the inner witness of God in the unbeliever's conscience) note the solo-sex implications obvious in "the lusts of their hearts" (v. 24), "vile passions" (v. 26), "debased mind" (v. 28) and "covetousness" (i.e., insatiable lust; v. 29). I have no question that those who relentlessly seek to avoid such accountability to conscience will always be able to find a way to license their own indulgence. But even here, God's Word is relentless, regularly speaking against *aselgeia* (for example, see Mark 7:22; Rom. 13:13; 2 Cor. 12:21; Gal. 5:19; and Eph. 4:19). Different versions of the Bible have translated this word in many different ways ("lasciviousness," "lewdness" and "wantonness" are some of the translations); and it is used to refer to the generally *unworthy*—that is, anything lacking value. The world may bypass this warning, but the inner witness of God's gift of conscience seeks to awaken in us this truth so that we might recover a sense of the *worthy*.

2. Solo sex panders to the spirit of lust.

The apostle Peter warned about the rise of lust to a point of dominative rule over many in the last days, adding a notation that mockers will decry righteousness: "Scoffers will come in the last days, walking according to their own lusts" (2 Pet. 3:3). Today's culture has not only abandoned the principles of sexual integrity according to the terms of God's Word, but also it *fosters* a replacement of sexual morality with the supposition that self-denial, or abstinence, is a waste of energy. (Even the term "sexually active," as contrasted with "sexually inactive," carries the implication that to deny oneself is to opt out of real life.) It is grieving to acknowledge, but disturbingly understandable as a sign of the times, that when this mood and this mind-set abound, solo sex becomes argued for by some in the Christian community. Meanwhile, with the ready availability of pornography—easily accessible in profusion as a means to stimulate and eventually bind believers in the chains of solo sex's fantasies—the way is wide open to inevitable complications brought by any moral compromise or corruption of the soul.

> When desire has conceived, it gives birth to sin; and sin, when it is full-grown, brings forth death (Jas. 1:15).

Having established in chapter 2 the seriousness with which Jesus regards the "look of lust," which is more than a glance but rather a mental investment of the mind in sexual interplay with the envisioned subject, we cannot escape confronting solo sex's usual partnership with fantasy and pornography. There is no reason to fool ourselves: Sexually provocative magazines are not purchased just for the sake of looking; they are millions of times a day opened and studied for the sake of fantasy during masturbation. Worse, as individuals give themselves to "fulfilling the desires of the flesh and of the mind" (Eph. 2:3) in the form of masturbation, demon spirits of this world are manipulating the situation. The dangers of submitting to the Adversary—by this

> # Masturbation and pornography are unholy partners in the Enemy's scheme to dethrone Jesus in a believer's life.

or any other means that "give[s] place to the devil" (Eph. 4:27)— are that even a momentary bonding of the mind with darkness puts a person in jeopardy of that brief encounter's becoming a long-term bondage. Masturbation and pornography are unholy partners in the Enemy's scheme to dethrone Jesus in a believer's life.

FINISHING THE COURSE IN TRIUMPH AND PURITY

Beloved, I beg you as sojourners and pilgrims, abstain from fleshly lusts which war against the soul.
1 PETER 2:11

Since Scripture calls us to lay aside those things that are not conducive to Christian growth, it ought to be incumbent upon us to care enough about the call of God to do that and, as the apostle Paul writes, to "press toward the goal for the prize of the upward call of God in Christ Jesus" (Phil. 3:14). As well, in Mark 4:18-19, Jesus' use of "thorns" as a picture of "the cares of this world, the deceitfulness of riches, and the desires for other things [that] . . . choke the word" is so picturesque an image of the piercing, penetrating, tearing power of lust. Our Lord concluded in noting how a life "becomes unfruitful" as the result (v. 19).

Paul's exhortation to his younger disciple-become-pastor, Timothy, included his call (and ours) to "flee . . . youthful lusts" (2 Tim. 2:22). I am not proposing that Paul had any specific lustful temptation in mind. However, who would deny—especially in today's sexually invasive (not merely permissive) culture—that the societal indifference toward the morally weakening practice of solo sex plays directly into patterns of other, more destructive indulgences? Frankly asked, Is there any more commonly acknowledged youthful lust than masturbation? It besets nearly everyone. Many of us, while fleeing from it as teenagers, fell flat on our faces. This doesn't justify it (or disqualify us), but if in faith we keep pressing toward the goal of the Spirit of the Lord, not the spirit of the world, we'll be able to overcome and say we've fought the fight and finished the course in triumph and purity.

DEFENDING YOUR HEART FOR GOD

How can we defend our hearts with regard to the world's mindset, which attempts to tilt our foundation in Christ toward that which is so far less than worthy or substantial?

First, take the subject of masturbation seriously. Take it seriously enough not to approve of it and not to argue in favor of it, seriously enough to acknowledge it as a problem and to confess it as a sin. We have made it clear that the believer practicing solo sex is not under God's condemnation. However, I know the majority feel convicted, as the Holy Spirit seeks to draw each of us forward into maturity and an overcoming lifestyle, and conviction needs to be responded to. Always remember, conviction and condemnation are two different things: *Conviction* is the Holy Spirit's summoning us to something better, indicating His grief over what isn't pleasing to Christ and His purpose to wean us away to the things that are the best for us as Jesus' followers. In

> ## A commitment to follow Jesus Christ involves answering His call to self-denial.

contrast, *condemnation* is an instrument of the Adversary, who will always seek to create doubt, or fear, that is calculated to drive you *away* from God; the Enemy's aim is to fixate your soul with uncertainty, or doubt, about His acceptance and love for you.

Second, don't permit the subject of masturbation to become a preoccupying concern or to become a barricade to good sense. As seriously as the subject deserves to be regarded, never respond with shock, criticalness or judgment when you hear about it. A reaction of shock will only deepen curiosity with a small child, beget fear and guilt with sensitive youth and possibly provoke rebellion with the young person who has confided in you. During the early teen years of a boy, occasional nocturnal emissions and other responses, if insensitively addressed, can result in an unnatural attitude about his body or his sexuality.

I have made clear that this chapter is *not* about confronting incidents born of self-discovery or about building a case for all Christian teachers of teens to introduce this theme as their "cause" or even to bother bringing it up publicly unless they are asked. My objective is to settle convictions concerning the Christian as a disciple and the fact that a commitment to follow (not simply put faith in) Jesus Christ involves answering His call to self-denial. My goal is that we overthrow casual attitudes about masturbation, not create the monstrosity of its becoming a sensationalized, laughed at, overdone subject among the youth in our churches. However, maturing young men and adults need to learn the biblical principle of discipleship: "When I became a man, I put away childish things" (1 Cor. 13:11).

If the habit of solo sex has been a struggling point in the life of someone you know or of someone who asks you for help, there are three steps to take that will bring progressive liberty and freedom.

1. Bring the problem to the Cross of Christ for cleansing; then, if necessary, seek the Cross's power to invoke deliverance from any residual bondage.

The Cross is the place where our forgiveness of all conscious sin and our deliverance from all lingering bondage have been provided. It is where we will find freedom from the past and hope for tomorrow (see Rom. 6:10-14; 1 John 1:9; Rev. 1:18).

2. Let Jesus' love cast out guilt, fear and tormenting thoughts.
Nothing gives place to the persistent power of temptation or to the devil's attempt to hold us in the grip of past habits like the fear of having "failed again." The pathway to abiding victory is often a see-saw, uphill-downhill, three-steps-forward-and-two-steps-back struggle. Don't let the struggles and challenges inher-

ent in the process of spiritual warfare become a point of despair. Rely on Jesus to keep on overcoming! While refusing to give your flesh comfort, don't fail to allow your soul to receive a generous amount of it. Jesus Christ comes in love to bring each of His disciples freedom from both crippling guilt and compromising carnality. Your acceptance before God is not because you've arrived at perfection but rather because you've chosen a direction: pursuing an overcoming life in Christ.

3. Press toward the things of the Spirit of God.

As you press toward the things of God, rest in the love He offers, which will assure your knowing the peace and satisfaction of all He intends for your life (see 1 John 4:18). Welcome the Holy Spirit as your Helper and Enabler as you pursue every part of your life as a disciple of Jesus. Let the living truth of God's Word become powerful in its promise for you that "if the Spirit of Him who raised Jesus from the dead dwells in you, He who raised Christ from the dead will also give life to your mortal bodies through His Spirit who dwells in you" (Rom. 8:11).

The Holy Spirit has come to "glorify Christ" and to do it in such a way that "Christ in you" becomes "the hope of glory" (Col. 1:27)—that is, God's promised certainty of victory in life and triumph over the flesh and the devil.

Dear one, take Jesus' promise to heart, and move forward in faith. He says: "If you abide in My word, you are My disciples indeed. And you shall know the truth, and *the truth shall make you free*" (John 8:31-32, emphasis added).

CHAPTER FIVE

RISING TO THE HEART'S DEFENSE

*For the weapons of our warfare are not carnal but mighty
in God for pulling down strongholds.*

2 CORINTHIANS 10:4

As we began this book, I related to you the account of an eight-year-old boy, innocently playing at a friend's home, completely unaware that a trap for his soul was being set. I described how that child—me—was mentally and emotionally affected at the moment when only two printed pages of pornographic writing were placed in his hand, with no pictures to tantalize, no videographic movement to dramatize, no audio to emphasize. They were only a few words and were rather mild by comparison with what is so common today.

Now, as we draw toward concluding our examination of the anatomy of seduction, I want to return to that story and elaborate how that internal, though momentary, upheaval became a snare to my young soul; how the Archdestroyer's seductive tactic attempted to lay the groundwork for the entrapment of a boy, then a teen, then a young man and ultimately *a life*. But I also want to tell you the end of that story: a "freeing" that didn't become discerned and unsnared until nearly 30 years after the trap had snapped on me in childhood's years.

Further, I want to secure in our minds the tormenting reality with which we began this book: the velvet-lined trap, the *satanic power* inherent in the abusive, the corrupt, the morally cheap, the sensually seductive or subtly stylized denigration of human sexuality that our society lauds—even as it weeps over human self-destructiveness. That satanic confusion explains the power that lurks behind the philosophically rationalized distorting of our human sexuality with the aim of seeking *first* to stun the soul, *later* to cripple its defenses and *finally* to completely destroy.

The subject of human bondage, especially where demonic influence is involved, is often confused (if acknowledged at all). The nature of Satan's ploys is addressed repeatedly in the Bible, yet Scripture's declaration that "we are not ignorant of his devices" (2 Cor. 2:11) is too often *not* the case with believers. Spiritual blindness, misinformation, insistence on human ways and supposed wisdom expose millions of people to certain bondage simply because they are either uninformed or willfully ignorant of God's truth.

Therefore my people have gone into captivity, because they have no knowledge; their honorable men are famished,

and their multitude dried up with thirst. Therefore Sheol
has enlarged itself and opened its mouth beyond measure
(Isa. 5:13-14).

It would be difficult to find a more graphic description of
what occurs when a person is seduced—caught in the velvet trap
of sexual seduction at any dimension, whether in the mind, the
emotions or the body—than Isaiah's. As Isaiah says, the emptiness
of carnal pursuits, however temporarily fulfilling, leaves even the
finest, the most "honorable," the most well-intentioned person
"famished." Thus deceived, he or she becomes one among the multitudes who are bound to pathways of relentlessly seeking carnal
gratification, deceived by having drunk at the fountain of lust—a
fountainhead that spews only hell's arid sands and leaves the
individual parched and plagued with an unquenchable thirst for
more, a thirst that can never be satisfied. That's the Bible's
description of the "captivity" that ignorance of and consequent
disobedience to God's Word bring about.

My personal story ends with a happier conclusion than
Isaiah's prophesied doom, though this cannot be attributed
either to me or to my strength of character. Being raised in a
home and environment that called a growing boy to Christ and
His ways made a massive difference in the atmosphere of the bat-
tlefield on which my soul was being contested. Steeled against a
mind-set of self-indulgence—especially where sexual compromise
was involved—I had an unquestionable advantage that braced me
against casual surrender to the temptations I faced in my teenage
years and during my early manhood. But at the same time, I was
exposed to all the resources with which our culture taunts and
seduces impressionable souls into the murky trench of temptation and compromise, as well all the curiosity and all the inclinations to toy with, or dabble in, the inappropriate.

And that's where my story resumes.

As I entered my teen years, like any young person I was regularly exposed to the banter of other kids whose stage of physical development and increasing social exposure to previously unavailable choices brought almost daily reference to the subject

> There is no lack of sexual snares in our twenty-first-century world. We are surrounded by a minefield of velvet-lined traps.

of sex. Keep in mind that this was decades ago, when proliferation of sexual imagery and hard-core porn—which so dehumanize sex and desensitize people—were *not* commonplace, as they are today. In my teen years, I was exposed to the ripple of whispers at school about reading a certain page of a book or the possibility of a forbidden thrill to be found by sending away to a post office box in another city for plain, brown-paper-wrapped trash.

Today, the temptations, their sources and resourcing are profoundly more abundant, more available, more explicit and more destructive. There is no lack of sexual snares in our twenty-first-century world. We are surrounded by a minefield of velvet-lined traps—some of which explode lives completely and others of which, like shrapnel, burrow into the soul's limbs to produce emotional or physical sexual dysfunction, crippling problems and various dimensions of personal pain for a lifetime.

Generally speaking, through those teen and college years, I

successfully navigated the majority of the traps that I encountered:

- the subtle suggestiveness of a female relative, luring me;
- the indirect but real offer by a high-school girlfriend at an enticing moment;
- the impulse to go out to pick up girls, which a dorm buddy and I nearly followed through on one evening;
- the flirtatious advance of a work associate when I was in college;
- the occasions of having pornographic material freely available.

All these were overcome through a combination of God's intervening mercies, my submission to the Holy Spirit's convictions and my inner resistance born of having been raised in a believing home and having committed my life to Christ. But I still faced those challenges and had to make my own decisions; the minefield was there, and the lures were set to attract my steps toward either explosive self-ruin or enslaving Enemy-laid snares.

Having learned sufficiently to *seek* God's gracious keeping power and having been faithfully *sustained* by His mercies, I came into marriage as a virgin. Yet I would later discover that even though sexual morality had been maintained, sexual pollution had gained a very real stronghold in my soul. Its snaring cords reached all the way back to that moment when I was eight.

While this bondage failed to find full expression because of my unwillingness to fully yield to habits that would compromise myself, I was still ongoingly haunted by an undiscerned "drawing." I would resist, presuming that the inclination was only of my own sinful potential, my flesh. I did not know that my path was being dogged by an evil spirit that was taunting me, relentlessly seeking for years to drag my soul backward and downward. The drawing was toward the pornographic. Though I never spent a single cent on pornography of any form, I understand pornography's effort at capturing the mind. Let me elaborate.

Drawn by Invisible Cords

For the first 20 years of my ministry, though I pastored my own church, I was constantly involved in speaking to and writing for young people. For five of those years, I served as the national director of youth for my denomination and spoke regularly to thousands of teens and collegians in camps and at conferences. And it was with a sincere desire to stay aware of those influences that were surrounding our culture and seeking to debilitate growth and maturity in budding young adults—not to mention corrupting their commitment as Christians—that I would pay attention to the content of contemporary music, films and books. I was wise enough not to be duped by the ignorant supposition that one has to experience everything in order to minister to those who have, so I generally only read reviews of new literature, films and music, or I would peruse books on the racks in airport shops or other public places while waiting for a flight or an appointment.

Strangely, I found myself having to exercise increasingly more willpower not to read further in a book that I was glancing through to verify what I had been told. It often required a strong, willful decision not to give in to the temptation to provide my eyes with the carnal feast provided by the centerfolds of magazines offering every exposure and the most corruptly inviting poses—all designed to leech the soul and lead to the heart's deception and bondage to emptiness, confusion and eventual corruption.

By describing the right decisions that I made, I do not intend to whitewash what I did. And though I never gave myself completely to what was imminently available, I know that I was nonetheless experiencing a bondage point that was waiting to build a wall of unholy, unhealthy sexual indulgence in my soul.

While not *pursuing* the corrupt, I was ongoingly drawn to it. And although the sense of "need to know" may or may not have been justified, I was blinded to the real nature of the drawing—a drawing by invisible cords that had been hooked into place so long before that I'd forgotten the incident. They were identified and severed only when I came to recognize them, in a moment that I still refer to as grace filled and miraculous.

Anna and I were residing for a full week at a beautiful hotel in the Midwest, comfortably housed there by the leaders who were hosting my ministry at their event. One afternoon, between my morning and evening sessions, we were both browsing at the hotel's gift shop and newsstand. I lifted a book from the rack of the general section, and with no awareness of its content, I opened its pages at random. Immediately I found myself confronted with what had to be the most lurid, crudely descriptive, disgustingly evil filth I had ever read. The only thing that took me beyond the first sentence (I stopped at the end of the second) was the disbelief that something so depraved could be found in a public place.

I literally was dizzied. I stood there a moment, reeling with the feeling that my arms and hands were dripping with foulness. In revulsion and disgust, I closed the book and returned it to the rack (placing it behind all the other books in that stack in order to distance it from ready availability).

I walked over to the counter where Anna was looking at some costume jewelry and said, "Honey, I just read the most awful thing I've ever read." I literally ached at having read those words, and right then and there I shared with Anna that I had made a pivotal decision.

Pornography Is "Ministered"

For we do not wrestle against flesh and blood, but against principalities, against powers, against the rulers of the darkness of this age, against spiritual hosts of wickedness in the heavenly places.

Ephesians 6:12

I was on the verge of discovering how real the power of pornography is and from what source that power is derived. Pornography is not just raw bodies or sex acts visually displayed, verbally related or editorially recounted in a book, magazine or film or on the Internet—offered up to the undiscerning soul to feed and excite the imagination. *Pornography is "ministered" by a spirit.* That spirit isn't named in the Bible, but it is unquestionably included among the "spiritual hosts of wickedness" mentioned in Ephesians 6:12, where God's Word expounds the prime movers in the spiritual warfare waged against every believer—indeed, all humanity. These are the dark powers under Satan's dominion.

The Scriptures clearly teach that idols are not merely sticks and stones, although they are nothing more than that in the natural realm; idolatry is a submission to demons (see 1 Cor. 10:19-21). In addition, the "imaginations" (2 Cor. 10:5, *KJV*; *logismoi* in the Greek) encountered in this spiritual war are "high things" (*hupsoma*) that arrogate to themselves what rightfully belongs to God:

Casting down imaginations, and every high thing that exalteth itself against the knowledge of God, and bringing

into captivity every thought to the obedience of Christ
(2 Cor. 10:5, *KJV*).

These high things oppose God's purpose in people and calculat-
ingly devise means for our defeat and destruction.

"Imaginations" is an excellent translation of "logismoi"
because it clearly conveys the idea of pornography. Indulgence in
pornography, therefore, becomes an idolatrous preoccupation,
commanding and dominating the mind and, in essence, receiving the worship of the devotee who soon becomes a prisoner—
usually not just to pornography but also to sensual bondage
that relentlessly cries out for more and more, each "more"
becoming more depraved than what preceded it.

The occurrence of "logismoi" in 2 Corinthians 10:5 evidences the place of imaginations as among those forces or
strategies manipulated by demonic powers. In the *New King
James Version* and the *New International Version* of the Bible, "imaginations" is translated as "arguments." This alternate translation, which may be defined as opposing ideas, could easily
obscure our insight into the horrendously evil nature of what
the apostle Paul made clear in this verse. In Gerhard Kittel's
Theological Dictionary of the New Testament, this word is discussed,
saying "These thoughts are not destroyed by carnal weapons,"[1]
thereby reminding us of the fact that they have become invested
with more than the power or force of human logic or dynamic.
This is because they connote "an emotional and volitional
emphasis [that] denotes a 'plan.' "[2] It doesn't take much discernment to figure out what the plan of demons is wherever human
beings give place to the demons' conniving—in this case, to
imaginations that steal the mind.

In actuality, all spiritual bondage is spread and administered
in the same way. It comes as a "word"—that is, an idea that may

move the mind or emotions to a disposition or an action or both. The motivating or dominating spirit behind that word *enables, actuates or enforces* behavior, and thereby lifestyle, and thus destiny. Similarly, the Holy Spirit of God's truth and power brings words. When He does, wisdom in living, blessing in life and glory eternally are the results. On the other hand, when a spirit that is under satanic dominion comes, the reverse is true. There is no middle ground. Every human thought or action, however innocently, inadvertently or casually expressed, finds its fountainhead in one kingdom or the other. It is important to lay this groundwork for our understanding, both to arrive at our goal of defending our hearts for God, as well as to adequately explain the profound discovery that I was about to make about myself.

THE SNARE IS REVEALED

The incident at the hotel newsstand that I described was not the first time I'd encountered this phenomenon of stopping at a magazine rack to browse through a book and then, opening it at random, discovering that I had "just happened" to land right in the middle of a sexually explicit scene. At one point, I remember hearing a gentle, corrective voice—one that I recognized wasn't mine—whispering deep inside me: "Why are you able to find it so easily?" I immediately put the book back on the shelf and left, yet I was still without full understanding of what was meant by the question or why it bothered me so much. Though I was disturbed by the emerging realization that the phenomenon was actually a *pattern*, it wasn't until the incident at the hotel that I began to face the question that I was hearing.

This time, I knew an important and absolute decision had to be made. Before Anna and I left that hotel, I prayed: "Father God, I will *never* open a book like that again. I will *never again* pick up a book that might have questionable content, as long as I live!" It was a moment of supreme decisiveness. Sobered by the incredibly foul material I had been led to, I drew a conclusion about the one who led me there. Let me illustrate.

Most Christians have experienced occasions in which they simply opened the Bible and discovered, to their amazement, that the passage they opened to spoke dramatically to their precise feelings or question of the moment. While this approach to the Scriptures should not be depended on, and certainly is not advocated by me as a means for divining immediate answers for life issues, it yet remains a fact that such moments have happened—probably to you. I mention this to propose why I believe this occurs: It is one means of God's providential dealings in our lives. *The Spirit that authored the Book knew where the passage was and in grace and kindness led you directly there!*

It was that conviction that caused me to become all the more sobered by the fact that I seemed to "just happen" on the vilest passages while I was casually looking over selections available at a newsstand, merely perusing books that I usually did not even know had unworthy content. Now, a deeper alert was resonating within my soul, and I wondered to myself if it might be that the "authoring spirit of darkness" behind such base literature was somehow finding a means of drawing me to its worst expression—hoping to tempt me, trap me and hold me in its trap.

The issue was finally settled. After years of rationalizing and justifying my habit as my seeking nothing more than a source of information to aid me in identifying with the people I was trying to reach, I made a clear-cut *renunciation* of such casual exposure to any written material I didn't recognize. Now that I finally understood *why* I could always find that "special page," I began moving toward my moment of deliverance. I hadn't even known that I'd needed deliverance, but my deliverance started that night; it began with my renunciation of my investigative habit (and to this day, I have never violated that vow).

Today, we are a long way from my era, when an eight-year-old child was snared by a few stolen pages of dirty writing. Most people reading this book have come up through adolescence and into adulthood and marriage surrounded by an availability of pornography. Any child, teen or adult *who is not even looking for pornography* needs only to tap a quick click on the Internet to

> In the culture of our time, defending our hearts for God from the perverting power of porn is nothing less than a full-time job.

suddenly become exposed to the most graphic trash imaginable, opening the door for lifelong confusion, personal struggle or bondage. Unquestionably, in the culture of our time, defending our hearts for God from the perverting power of porn is nothing less than a full-time job. At the core, this responsibility and the power of choice to exercise it reside within each of us—at least until a soul becomes so bound by the Adversary that the surrender of the will's power to resist has been broken.

We choose—each of us—what it is we allow into our thoughts when we are confronted by the unworthy, and we each also choose whether we will dwell on a thought, stay on a TV channel, keep a website open or continue reading a book or magazine. Allowing things that we know are less than contributive to right and worthy purposes into our lives is a concession that the

Adversary will snag on, and thus the Word's command: "[Do not] give place to the devil. And do not grieve the Holy Spirit" (Eph. 4:27,30).

In contrast to surrender, we are called to "resist the devil" (Jas. 4:7). God promises us in James 4:7-10 that if we make that choice, the devil will flee from us and that such faithful submission to God, by means of obedience, repentance and renunciation, assures the pathway to victory. It's the way to keep from stumbling into a snare, and it holds the precious benefit of increased intimacy with God, for in resisting the devil the way is being pursued to "draw near to God and He will draw near to you" (v. 8).

HOW DELIVERANCE IS ACCOMPLISHED

I have shared within these pages two deeply personal stories: one with regard to how the Holy Spirit revealed a snare of pornography that lodged in my soul as an eight-year-old, and the other with regard to how He delivered me from an entrapment that surely would have led to adultery. With this, let me set in place a pathway of freedom that can be found by all who either know they are bound by a sexual habit of some kind or who may suspect that possibility.

You may have never even considered this, for you—like me—have not made any direct concession or surrender with a conscious commitment to evil but have been deceived or deluded or have wandered into a trap. Or, perhaps you have not been victimized yourself, but you know someone whom you might be able to help, because that person is open and ready to seek God's intervening grace in his or her situation. So let me provide helpful insights that I have grown to understand, personally and pastorally: first, insight into *what we mean by "deliverance"*; and second, *how a person may receive freedom from spiritual bondage.*

WHAT WE MEAN BY "DELIVERANCE"

Everything of our salvation provided for in Christ entails *deliverance*! Let this *first* fact become settled in your mind: "Deliverance" is not only a biblical term, but it is also a divine process. It is a glorious word describing the full impact of the gospel at the expanded dimensions of our being; it is not a separate commodity or a peculiar oddity of doctrine. Deliverance is *the essence of* all aspects of our salvation, not only *a feature within* it. The Word of God declares this threefold deliverance in many ways, but none so succinctly as 2 Corinthians 1:10: "[God] *delivered* us from so great a death, and *does deliver* us; in whom we trust that He *will still deliver us*" (emphasis added). Please note this deliverance:

1. We *have been delivered* from the *penalty* of sin—its shame, guilt, stain and condemnation. This refers to our regeneration and justification in Christ—the certainty and securing of our eternal place within God's grace.

2. We *are being delivered* from the *power* of sin—its grip, its rule, its habit, its disease, its dominion. This refers to our ongoing growth in the Word; increase in God's righteous ways; and through the Holy Spirit's processes of sanctification, freedom from (a) any bondages residual to our past or yielded to as a believer (see Rom. 6:3-14,16), unto (b) a steadfastness in refusing to give place to the flesh—the old man—which is to be refused any place of governance in our

lives or choices (see Gal. 5:16-21; Eph. 4:17-24).

3. We *will be delivered* from the *presence* of sin—death,
   destruction and all that is in the world—at the coming of Jesus, forever! This refers to the joyous hope
   that at Jesus' coming for His Church, we shall be
   taken into His presence forever—never again to be
   taunted by the world's carnal devices, by our own sinful flesh or by the devil (see 1 Cor. 15:50-58; Titus
   2:13-14).

Hear me, dear one: the scope of your salvation and mine is
broad, deep and thoroughgoing. The key Hebrew and Greek words
used in the Bible for "to save" entail the concept of deliverance:

- yasha (Hebrew)—to save, to open, to free, to rescue
- sozo (Greek)—to save, to deliver, to protect

With these basic words of salvation, others are added in both the
Old Testament and New Testament, as illustrated by the following examples (emphasis added to each):

- palat (Hebrew, in Ps. 18:2)
  "The LORD is my rock and my fortress and my *deliverer;*
  my God, my strength, in whom I will trust."
- peleytah (Hebrew, in Obad. 17)
  "But on Mount Zion there shall be *deliverance*, and
  there shall be holiness; the house of Jacob shall possess
  their possessions."
- rhuomai (Greek, in Matt. 6:13; see also Luke 11:4)
  "And do not lead us into temptation, but *deliver* us
  from the evil one. For Yours is the kingdom and the
  power and the glory forever. Amen."

• exaireo (Greek, in Gal. 1:4-5)

"Who [our Lord Jesus Christ] gave Himself for our sins, that He might *deliver* us from this present evil age, according to the will of our God and Father, to whom be glory forever and ever. Amen."

Still, to focus the breadth of our deliverance is not to withdraw from the more specific use of the word as it bears on the breaking of satanic oppression or demonic bondage. Deliverance in this regard has to do with the freeing of individuals from torment, suffering or affliction; from the things that inhibit joyful or fruitful living, or manifest restrictive bonds in thoughts, attitudes or habits. These points of bondage occur or take root in innumerable ways, but the constant is our Adversary's readiness to invade terrain in the soul that is either granted by repeated *known* disobedience or forfeited by recurrent wandering in ignorance or even blinded innocence. So, in our present discussion, what I mean by "deliverance" specifically addresses those bondages to sexual indulgence of any kind that have come about through conscious surrender to a practice or (as with my experience as a child) through innocent exposure to a nonetheless hateful work of darkness. These are situations in which the specific sense of "breaking the bonds of demonic oppression" needs application.

While the following biblical cases do not directly deal with sexual bondage, they demonstrate how the grip of the Adversary becomes established in part of a person's life and how Jesus Christ comes to set a person—*all of us!*—free. Jesus is able to accomplish this in the following situations:

• *Where the source of a sickness or affliction is demonic*
The Lord Jesus said, "So ought not this woman, being

a daughter of Abraham, whom Satan has bound—
think of it—for eighteen years, be loosed from this
bond on the Sabbath?" (Luke 13:16). The text speaks of
"a spirit of infirmity" (v. 11) and thus designates this
specific activity of the devil. Of course, this neither
teaches nor should it be concluded that all sickness is
demonic in origin or that it is a direct result of an individual's sinning.

- *Where a residue of the past lifestyle is still dominant*
Peter said, "Repent therefore of this your wickedness,
and pray God if perhaps the thought of your heart may
be forgiven you. For I see that you are poisoned by bit-
terness and bound by iniquity" (Acts 8:22-23). The context (see vv. 13-21) reveals that Simon had believed and
had been baptized, but that the spirits that enabled his
past involvement in sorcery were now seeking to sustain their control through him by extending his former
self-serving, control-of-others lifestyle.

- *Where a believer may consciously open himself or herself to
satanic influence through willful disobedience, indulgence or
rebellion*
"Therefore, putting away lying . . . 'be angry, and do
not sin' . . . nor give place to the devil" (Eph. 4:25-27).
The entire context is a summons away from the traits of
worldly indulgence. The word "place" (*topos*) clearly
indicates a specific possibility of the surrender of a location in the soul of a believer, which may come under the
influence of the world-spirit, which fosters the behavior
that is willfully given place to in the believer's life.

- *Where a regression to past attitudes and practice is allowed*
"But now after you have known God, or rather are
known by God, how is it that you turn again to the

weak and beggarly elements, to which you desire again to be in bondage?" (Gal. 4:9). The word *stoicheia* (Greek for "elements") refers to more than merely the patterns, or the ABCs, of the world's way or philosophy. Translators and other scholars probe the depths of this word, and Greek lexicons describe its use when referring to those demons who energize a culture's animistic or folk religions. The text hereby is referencing how dark spirits move in the midst of activities that substitute or detract from the worship of the One, True and Living God, exploiting human exposures to bondage by reason of their excursions from God's divine order. Thus, they invade and establish strongholds of control in people, having been given "legal right" to occupy a place in the soul by reason of sin or of blindness to sin's consequences.

Thus, by "deliverance" I am referring to

- that aspect of the finished work of Jesus Christ's Cross,
- by which He has broken the power of the Evil One and
- by which any work or entrenchment to his dark kingdom
- in oppressing or tormenting one of the Lord's redeemed
- may be vanquished, dissolved or expelled
- by the authority of the believer in Christ who is standing in their identity in Him
- and who is extending the triumph of the Name of Jesus and the Blood of His Cross.

To summarize then, an acknowledgment that satanic oppression or bondage may be present within a believer is not to provide anyone with an excuse from responsibility for their own actions. The cheap, worn escape clause "The devil made me do it" won't work! Each of us who sins is completely responsible for our own actions, whatever the motivation or energy behind it. To deal with the issue of deliverance is not to suggest a shallow attitude toward sin or a convenient exit from personal responsibility. But I do long to help people discover two truths.

First, not all sinning or recurrent failure that a believer seeks to overcome is necessarily of the flesh alone. While self-will (fleshly mindedness) may be the beginning point of surrender to sin, there are times when sin gives place to the devil. When that occurs, the Adversary's "occupational force" may take hold and gain dominion. When bondage is in place, deliverance is needed. Efforts at self-discipline, however noble, may momentarily stand but will cave in beneath the power of the Adversary. As I often say, "You can't 'cast out' flesh, but neither can you 'discipline' a demon."

Second, where bondage is identified and confronted, the will and the Word of God submitted to and the principles outlined here applied, *deliverance is available and victory is certain!* There is a freedom waiting for any bound soul as "they may come to their senses and escape the snare of the devil, having been taken captive by him to do his will" (2 Tim. 2:26).

Bondage *always* exists because of disobedience and sin. However, some instances that bring bondage to human souls are not consciously perceived at the time the evil becomes locked into place. This was the case with what happened to me as a boy with regard to the spirit of pornography. Similarly, many bondages are put into place during the years of a person's living distant from God's ways; they become entrenched in habit or attitude, but Christ, as the Light of the World within them, now seeks to burn those bondages away through the processes of the Holy Spirit's effecting their sanctification.

Now, the Rest of the Story

On that morning in my childhood when I was at my friend's house and his older brother offered us a brief two pages of a lewd story, we didn't know that what we were about to read was pornographic, because he had told us, "This is something funny." Not only wasn't it, but also what eventuated that day was the success of a cruel satanic "joke," which was so cleverly delivered that I didn't know a calculated trap had caught my young soul. Proverbs 1:17 explains how a net laid to entrap a creature will not succeed if the creature sees it being set. But in my childhood innocence, I simply did not see what was happening at the moment. I only felt the flush of mixed surprise, an awakened desire for the illicit and a fearful sense of having transgressed a boundary. The headiness of the moment—literally, being dizzied and heated by an unholy fire—was registering a strategic success by a spirit, though I understood nothing of this at the time. However, I was about to discover the fact that a snare had snapped shut and that its teeth would attempt to grind up my soul in years to come.

Years later, at the hotel newsstand in Illinois, I renounced my habit of opening questionable reading material at random. About three weeks after I did, I was alone in my office back home in California, kneeling in prayer. As I prayed for various matters, I was moved to give myself to a focused season of prayer in the Spirit, allowing the Holy Spirit to assist my intercession beyond the limits of my own human knowledge.[3]

At the moment, I had been praying for matters pertaining to ministry issues at our church, coming events, staff and member needs—not even thinking about the subject that was about to surface. Then, the Lord seemed to bring my attention back to that moment weeks before at the newsstand, when I had made my decision and my verbal renunciation.

As I continued this Holy Spirit-enabled prayer, a stark yet soon-to-be-liberating revelation came to mind: It was as though a reel of film were being projected before my eyes and as though I were standing high above a room, watching two young boys who were seated, bent over a game they were playing. A slightly older boy entered and handed them some folded papers, which the two younger boys opened and began to read. Suddenly I became aware of what I was being shown—one of those little boys was *me!* I had been drawn by another Spirit (whose "name" is *Holy*), my understanding taken back over three decades to an incident that had been completely lost to my conscious mind but that now brought back the recollection of how mentally and emotionally impacting that moment had been.

Then, simultaneous with my "vision," a whisper breathed into my mind, saying, *"Pornography."* I intuitively knew the source of the whisper, for it was spoken with such *strength and comfort;* I was aware it was the Comforter, the Holy Spirit, present in power as He showed me (1) that the source of the lifetime drawing power was a spirit that "ministers" pornography; and (2) that in that very moment of prayer, He would glorify our Lord Jesus' power to deliver me—to once and for all *break* the stronghold that had so long taunted and haunted my mind!

A joyous spirit of faith and praise swept over me: I not only rejoiced in the confidence of a victory at hand, but I also applied a set of principles I had earlier come to understand as *keys* for a person's being loosed from spiritual bondage.

FOUR LIBERATING KEYS

Over years of teaching and ministering God's beautiful and liberating Word of Truth on issues of human sexuality, I have spoken in public services to innumerable thousands—often to as many as 50,000 men at a time and not uncommonly to as many as 2,000 men and women together. When coming to the conclusion of a teaching, the most demanding moment comes at the point of decision: *What are you going to do about what you have discovered—about God, yourself, His Word and your future?*

And so I ask you, *As you and I have shared together via these pages, what has He shown you?* What has God surfaced to your understanding or convicted you about concerning your past or present practices, or concerning what He is pressing you to take an unswerving stance toward?

I regularly conclude teaching by outlining a set of four keys to personal breakthrough, four principles that follow on the heels of our coming to honestly face up to the Holy Spirit's dealings. These four keys, which form a pathway of action-unto-sexual freedom—in other words, how we can defend our hearts for God—all begin with the letter *R:* "*Repentance,*" "*Renunciation,*" "*Recitation*" and "*Release.*" These principles will become effective when a full-hearted, absolute and total response is given to the revelation of the Word of God—not only to its *content*, but also to its specific implications—to the things the Holy Spirit has *shown you.* That's the "revelation" that takes place when His Word of Truth confronts us and comes alive to our understanding, and we allow it to penetrate the inmost secret parts of our souls. When you or I are ready to yield *that* response, Christ is ready and gloriously able to bring full forgiveness, deliverance and peace and to open a new pathway of freedom before us.

Before you begin, you may wish to pray a prayer for inviting the Lord to fill you with the Holy Spirit (see appendix 2). If you have simply sought resource here for ministry to others and have secured strength and stability in the sexual integrity of your own life, I believe you also will find these principles practical and useful in teaching and leading others.

Repentance

Repentance involves the response of an awakened mind that says, *Without reserve, I turn from my way to Yours, Lord.* It is the result of a doubly enlightened heart; one that sees the awfulness of its sin and the sin's destructive evil and that lifts its eyes to see the wonderful love and mercy of our dear Jesus Christ and His readiness to establish His Kingdom power and freedom within us (see Heb. 4:14-16).

> Repentance involves the response of an awakened mind that says, *Without reserve, I turn from my way to Yours, Lord.*

To give a personal example, I repented while at the newsstand, when I came to the realization that my habit of reviewing books—even if being relatively harmless in comparison to purchasing or pursuing the pornographic and even if discovering passages of books "accidentally"—was nonetheless the result of my having *given place* to patterns of behavior I now saw as completely unworthy of any of my time, whatever the rationale. I *turned* from my way of human wisdom and habit to acknowledge the Father's will and Christ's way for me instead.

Renunciation

Renunciation involves a decisive declaration that makes no defense of any aspect of our sin, habit or bondage. No place in the heart or mind is tolerated as a private reserve, and Romans

13:14 is activated as we "make no provision for the flesh, to fulfill its lusts." In the Old Testament, renunciation was characterized by removing one's coat and tearing it in half or by taking ashes or the dust of the ground and pouring it over one's head. Its purpose was *to treat the sin with the scorn it deserved—to take nothing of it lightly and to openly reject and renounce all of it, completely.*

Following the newsstand awakening of my sensitivity to the unworthiness of my habit, however harmless I had perceived it to be, I declared it *hateful* and *unholy, a concession to my flesh that I would never again allow.* I renounced my rationalized reviewings as inexcusable on any terms and in total violation of anything of God's ways for my life.

Recitation

Recitation involves *specific* confession of sins, and it is a principle I have found to be pivotally important in taking steps to rid us of imprinted memories that attempt to haunt the soul. The Bible says, "If we confess our sins, He is faithful and just to forgive us our sins and to cleanse us from all unrighteousness" (1 John 1:9). This text notes "sins" (plural)—the itemizing of the details of past failure, *not* because God is calling us to grovel in shame, but because He is seeking to *dismantle* the stronghold of ensconced memories that will return to plague us later if the sins are only generalized by a "forgive me of all my sin" prayer.

In my case, as the vision of myself as a child unfolded, I prayed through each aspect of what was now being made clear to my understanding. From the many times I had counseled others toward deliverance in their own lives, I knew that recitation involves speaking out everything the Lord brings to mind—unedited and in detail—and bringing the whole event before the Cross and placing it under the Blood of Jesus Christ. So I did that: I "walked through" the memory of how the inner explosion of lust had occurred; how the dizziness had come over me (I believe it was the moment the spirit found a foothold in my soul); and how I later laughed at what we had read—feeling smugly grown-up—even though I felt guilt and shame and knew even then that I should have asked for God's forgiveness.

Making a complete confession, I spoke aloud in prayer to the Lord all I could remember about the scene that He was helping me see again. I did so knowing that it was His Spirit at work, showing me what He did because it was my moment of available freedom. He was freeing me from *each and all* of the implications of those things that had become attached to me as a little boy: the place *lust* was allowed through my not stopping when I was reading; the place *pornography* found as an immediate result; the place *pride* was given when two boys would later think themselves to be smart for having gained carnal knowledge.

The disentangling power of a full confession is part of the process of deliverance, but it is important to distinguish this exercise of confession of sins from another, and most foundational, point of confession. Be clear, dear one, that unless the Holy Spirit brings it about in individual cases at conversion, such detail is *not* essential when a person comes to receive Christ as Savior. To be born again, we only need to turn to Christ, from our selves and *sin,* acknowledging our dependence on His Cross and on the saving, cleansing Blood to justify us before God and to forgive our sin. However, the growth process the Bible calls sanctification includes such moments of profound and broken humble confession of *sins* as we experience the ongoing refinement and purification of the Holy Spirit's presence in our lives, which brings holiness of life, spiritual freedom and Christlikeness in character.

Release

Release comes through the interaction of God's Word and the Holy Spirit's application of it as we open to Him in faith and with a spirit of praise. See it in the Scriptures, dear one:

- God's Word is a source of liberation—"You shall know the truth, and the truth shall make you free" (John 8:32).
- God's Spirit comes to minister that liberation—"The Lord is the Spirit; and where the Spirit of the Lord is, there is liberty" (2 Cor. 3:17).

God's Word and His Holy Spirit bind together to loose the soul; they blend together to break bondage; and they unite together to undo what flesh and devils have conspired to extract of hope, health and peace from our lives. As the Word is applied and the Spirit welcomed, then *let the spirit of faith and praise arise!* Faith is our means of accepting what is ours through Christ's Cross; praise is our means of overthrowing all adversarial claims of sin or dark powers. Exalt Jesus! Glorify Him for what He offers, for what He has promised and for what He is doing, even now as you pray!

I described how I was overtaken with a spirit of faith and praise. Why can we rejoice? Because whom the Son sets free is free indeed (see John 8:36), and the same release I experienced is available to all who read these words, irrespective of what it is they've known, done, been bound by or been afraid to believe would ever be broken.

The Bible says that the Holy Spirit, who dwells in us, is jealous for total dominion in our lives (see Jas. 4:5). In fact, in the *King James Version* of the Bible, the words used for "jealousy" in that passage of Scripture are "lusteth to envy," underscoring the

Holy Spirit's emphatic passion that He will allow *nothing* to dominate our lives or cripple our capacities as potential representatives of Christ our Lord and of the Kingdom of God. So I warmly but boldly affirm that truth, as we conclude these pages together, inviting you to seize the promise in these truths—in the four *R*s detailed above. Take them and apply them as you minister to others, or if you need to, apply them at any point in your own life.

If there is anything being awakened to your own understanding, any point of confrontation the Spirit of God may be bringing to your own heart, don't hestitate. In simple, childlike obedience, bring it to the Lord Jesus—*now*. Bring all you might remember about a time in your past or a problem in your present. Bring it all to the Lord and place it under the Blood of His Cross, exposing every detail of anything Satan could use in his attempt to sustain dominion over any part of your life.

You may want to pray,

> *Lord, by the power of the Blood of Calvary and in the Name of Jesus, I sever every point of bondage* [take time to address each with repentance and passionate renunciation].
> *I break every oppressive yoke, and I receive the freedom that only You can give from every point where I have surrendered to carnal indulgence or have given place to any dark power that may have gained a foothold in me.*

Then, as the Holy Spirit reveals and releases you from bondage points, begin to give thanks and praise the Lord Jesus. Be free to speak—indeed, to sing or to shout—a bold declaration of His forgiveness of your sin.

Remember, dear one, God is never shocked by the specifics of our human failure; but He is aware of how tendrils of sin—

each with its own gripping, grasping power—seek to retain their influence on our thoughts and habits and to disturb deep inner peace, even by the subtlety of satanic taunts that may hammer at the corners of our psyches. So whether ministering to another or coming in prayer for yourself, God invites us to "come boldly to the throne of grace, that we may obtain mercy and find grace to help in time of need" (Heb. 4:16). With that, He assures us that "If we confess our sins, He is faithful and just to forgive us our sins and to cleanse us from all unrighteousness" (1 John 1:9). To assist you in that, a prayer for renouncing sex sin and inviting deliverance may be found in appendix 3.

WALK IN GOD'S EXPANDING LIBERTY

If anything in my testimony rings familiar, the same solutions that delivered me from a snare can deliver any sincere believer who desires liberty. Feeding on the Word and praying in the Spirit are disciplines that we must build into our lives. As we feed on the Word, pray in partnership with the Holy Spirit and walk in obedience and purity while refusing to surrender to the world-spirit of seduction and deception, the Holy Spirit will lead us into continually expanding freedom.

We began this book by talking about the velvet-lined trap of temptation. The Bible does not say that we will never be tempted; rather, it says that

> No temptation has overtaken you except such as is common to man; but God is faithful, who will not allow you to be tempted beyond what you are able, but with the temptation will also make the way of escape, that you may be able to bear it. Therefore, my beloved, flee from idolatry (1 Cor. 10:13-14).

To take a defensive posture against temptation, against those things that seduce and snare, means that we "flee from idolatry"—from those indulgences that enthrone self over our Savior and that invite satanic oppression and bondage.

We who have been given new life and forgiveness of sin are admonished by the Word of God to "stand fast therefore in the liberty by which Christ has made us free, and do not be entangled again with a yoke of bondage" (Gal. 5:1). Discipleship mandates that once we have been delivered from the snares of seduction, we do not give place to them again. My hope for all who read this book is that, having exposed the anatomy of seduction by means of both biblical grounds and practical application, you will close these pages equipped, enabled and empowered to stand your ground with the authority our Lord tells us to invoke:

> Do not lead us into temptation, but deliver us from the evil one. For Yours is the kingdom and the power and the glory forever (Matt. 6:13).

To which I say, *"Amen!"*

A PRAYER FOR RECEIVING CHRIST AS LORD AND SAVIOR

It seems possible that some earnest inquirer may have read this book and somehow still never have received Jesus Christ as personal Savior. If that's true of you—that you have never personally welcomed the Lord Jesus into your heart to be your Savior and to lead you in the matters of your life—I would like to encourage you and help you to do that.

There is no need to delay, for an honest heart can approach the loving Father God at any time. So I'd like to invite you to come with me, and let's pray to Him right now.

If it's possible there where you are, bow your head, or even kneel if you can. In either case, let me pray a simple prayer first and then I've added words for you to pray yourself.

MY PRAYER

Father God, I have the privilege of joining with this child of Yours who is reading this book right now. I want to thank You for the openness of heart being shown toward You and I want to praise You for Your promise, that when we call to You, You will answer.

I know that genuine sincerity is present in this heart, which is ready to speak this prayer, and so we come to You in the Name and through the Cross of Your Son, the Lord Jesus. Thank you for hearing.[1]

And now, speak your prayer.

YOUR PRAYER

Dear God, I am doing this because I believe in Your love for me, and I want to ask You to come to me as I come to You. Please help me now.

First, I thank You for sending Your Son, Jesus, to Earth to live and to die for me on the Cross. I thank You for the gift of forgiveness of sin that You offer me now, and I pray for that forgiveness.

Forgive me and cleanse my life in Your sight, through the Blood of Jesus Christ. I am sorry for anything and everything I have ever done that is unworthy in Your sight. Please take away all guilt and shame, as I accept the fact that Jesus died to pay for all my sins and through Him, I am now given forgiveness on this earth and eternal life in heaven.

I ask You, Lord Jesus, please come into my life now. Because You rose from the dead, I know You're alive and I want You to live with me—now and forever.

I am turning my life over to You and from my way to Yours. I invite Your Holy Spirit to fill me and lead me forward in a life that will please the heavenly Father.

Thank You for hearing me. From this day forward, I commit myself to Jesus Christ, the Son of God. In His name, amen.[2]

A PRAYER FOR INVITING THE LORD TO FILL YOU WITH THE HOLY SPIRIT

Dear Lord Jesus,

I thank You and praise You for Your great love and faithfulness to me.

My heart is filled with joy whenever I think of the great gift of salvation You have so freely given to me,

And I humbly glorify You, Lord Jesus, for You have forgiven me all my sins and brought me to the Father.

Now I come in obedience to Your call.

I want to receive the fullness of the Holy Spirit.

I do not come because I am worthy myself, but because You have invited me to come.

Because You have washed me from my sins, I thank You that You have made the vessel of my life a worthy one to be filled with the Holy Spirit of God.

I want to be overflowed with Your life, Your love and Your power, Lord Jesus.

I want to show forth Your grace, Your words, Your goodness and Your gifts to everyone I can.

And so with simple, childlike faith, I ask You, Lord, fill me with the Holy Spirit. I open all of myself to You to receive all of Yourself in me.

I love You, Lord, and I lift my voice in praise to You.
I welcome Your might and Your miracles to be manifested in me for
  Your glory and unto Your praise.

I'm not asking you to say "amen" at the end of this prayer, because after inviting Jesus to fill you, it is good to begin to praise Him in faith. Praise and worship Jesus, simply allowing the Holy Spirit to help you do so. He will manifest Himself in a Christ-glorifying way, and you can ask Him to enrich this moment by causing you to know the presence and power of the Lord Jesus. Don't hesitate to expect the same things in your experience as occurred to people in the Bible. The spirit of praise is an appropriate way to express that expectation; and to make Jesus your focus, worship as you praise. Glorify Him and leave the rest to the Holy Spirit.

A Prayer for Renouncing Sex Sin and Inviting Deliverance

Prayer

Heavenly Father, I come to you in the Name of Jesus. I come with repentance and humility to receive the cleansing I need. I believe the Blood of Jesus cleanses me from all sin. Holy God, I desire cleansing and freedom from all sexual sin and impurity and all unholy soul ties.* I confess and repent of my own sexual sins and of the sexual sins of my former generations.**

I specifically confess as sin and I repent of giving place to sexual lust: lust of the eyes, lust of the flesh, impure thoughts and all sexual fantasies.

I repent for all involvement with any kind of pornography. I specifically repent of the viewing or use of pornographic photos, books or magazines, pornographic movies, computer pornography and Internet chat rooms.

I repent of all involvement in the sins of fornication, adultery, infidelity and prostitution. I repent of all involvement in perverted sex, including homosexuality, sodomy, sadism, orgies, group sex and sexual activity with animals.

Heavenly Father, I specifically repent of all attitudes and all words or actions forcing or requiring my spouse to participate or take part in any sexual acts which to them are degrading and distasteful or which violate their conscience before God.

I repent of sexual self-gratification and self-indulgence, including masturbation, exhibitionism and Internet or telephone sex. I also repent of all attitudes, actions and spirits associated with sexual pride, sexual power, sexual conquest, enticement and seduction.

And now, Father God, I renounce*** all these sexual sins: all sexual immorality, fornication and adultery, lust of the flesh, perversion, pornography, sexual abuse, selfishness and manipulation. I renounce all unclean spirits behind these sins. I renounce all unholy soul ties. I want nothing more to do with them or with any sexual sin, in the Name of Jesus.

In the Name of Jesus, through the power of the Holy Spirit, I break the yoke of bondage from all sexual sins. I choose from this moment on to walk sexually pure before my God.[1]

DEFINITIONS

*Soul Ties

A mental or emotional attachment of the soul to a person or object, involving both the mind and emotions, resulting in the influencing of the choices of our will.

There are *good soul ties* (see Gen. 2:24; 44:30; Deut. 10:20; 1 Sam. 18:1; and 2 Sam. 20:2) and *destructive soul ties* (see Gen. 34:1-3; Num. 25:1-3; Josh. 23:12-13; and 1 Cor. 6:16).

**Generational Ties

Keeping mercy for thousands, forgiving iniquity and transgression and sin, by no means clearing the guilty, visiting the iniquity of the fathers upon the children and the children's children to the third and the fourth generation.

EXODUS 34:7

Although the sins of former generations are not credited to our account, there is still something very destructive that takes place. If the sins of our parents are unrepented of, the spiritual influence behind those sins tends to press in on us in the next generation (i.e., children of abusive parents are more likely to succumb to abusive behavior in their own life).

***Renouncing

The night is far spent, the day is at hand. Therefore let us cast off the works of darkness, and let us put on the armor of light.

ROMANS 13:12

And have no fellowship with the unfruitful works of darkness, but rather expose them.

EPHESIANS 5:11

An action taken by the believer in Jesus Christ against the forces of darkness that declares all previous association to be canceled. All words, agreements or actions that opened the door to demonic influence are now broken.

REGARDING QUESTIONS ABOUT ORAL AND ANAL SEX

Given the preoccupation of today's culture, in which sexual gratification has become a substitute goal for true sexual responsibility, integrity and highest marital fulfillment, questions are regularly asked of me concerning oral and anal sex, including questions about the personal or partnering use of devices designed to artificially stimulate or substitute for normal sexual intercourse. Rather than deal with this within the body of this book, I am offering in this appendix the essential counsel I have provided when couples voluntarily inquire of me regarding oral sex. My remarks presume an understanding that homosexual behavior is not intended for humankind, nor is it biblically supported.

By "oral sex," I refer to the practice of the mouthing of the penis (fellatio) or vagina (cunnilingus). Like masturbation, oral sex has been supposed by some unmarried believers as a means of preserving chastity. Further, oral sex has come to be broadly regarded within society as "not really sex." A number of years ago, this monumental delusion, which opposes all truth, gained national reinforcement from an American president. In testimony related to a legal case, our government's highest official declared that, with regard to his sexual involvement with a female intern, he did not consider the act of oral sex to be "sex."

In the years since that national humiliation, this deception has seeped like a virus into the mind-set of an alarming number of middle-school- and high-school-aged teenagers who do not consider either performing or having oral sex performed on them to be a sexual act. This fraud has become so pervasive and entrenched that parents interviewed recently on *The Oprah Winfrey Show* said that their teens tell them that oral sex "is like a kiss" and that it's "no big deal because everybody is doing it." The parents went on to explain that this act is sometimes openly performed in view of other kids.[1] The peer pressure to act out in this degrading manner also reveals the disturbing low self-esteem of so many young girls in today's society.

As a thought-provoking sidebar to the issue of sexuality among teens, a study released in 2003 by the National Campaign to Prevent Teen Pregnancy concluded that adults underestimate their influence on teens and that teenagers want more advice from their parents on sex.[2] But questions about oral sex (and masturbation) are so frequently asked of our church's pastoral staff by both married believers as well as by engaged couples that the readiness of many of today's parents and churches to answer teens' questions seems sadly lacking—both of convictions about and of commitment to teaching people about sexual self-discipline. Private counsel with these individuals and couples too often turns up deep personal problems stemming from these inordinate practices.

SEXUAL COMMUNICATION IN MARRIAGE

Marriage is honorable among all, and the bed undefiled; but fornicators and adulterers God will judge. Let your conduct be without covetousness; be content with such things as you have.

HEBREWS 13:4-5

The perversion that has overtaken our society with practices and lifestyles akin to homosexual behavior ought to be a concern for believers seeking to pursue a godly relationship within their marriages. Both oral and anal sex are now considered fairly acceptable behaviors within marriage. Yet I have never been in a counseling situation in which I've found that either of these practices contributed to the fulfillment of the marriage. Instead, I have dealt with many, many cases in which they have distracted from the highest satisfaction of the husband and wife's union.

The Bible does not specifically say that oral and anal sex are disallowed in a marriage relationship. But in Hebrews 13:4, it does say that the marriage bed is to be *kept* "undefiled"—a mandate stating that couples must preserve their love life, not only for one another, but also free of the world's corrupting influence. For example, pornographic videos are not to model lovemaking for a believing couple. The world's preoccupation with orgasmic gratification at any cost is opposed to the biblical model of sexual fulfillment begotten in a climate of honor, mutual devotion to one another, loving communication and even fiery passion. The call given to believing couples in Hebrews 13:4 to practice the self-imposed discipline of keeping their marriage lovemaking untainted by the cheap ways of the world is not a call to something less than high desire or spontaneity; rather, it is a call, even within the freed and freeing arena of the married sexual relationship, to maintain vigilance against anything that gradually introduces impurity and ultimately reduces vitality. So it is that the New Testament instruction points married disciples to a sensitivity and availability to the Holy Spirit's promptings to *keep their marriage bed (i.e., sexual intimacies) unpolluted*—free of the things that dissipate that pure energy for the preciousness of the face-to-face communication and overwhelming ecstatic and satisfying union our Creator designed this aspect of our humanity to enjoy.[3]

Sexual communication within a marriage is equally as important as verbal communication. Throughout nearly 50 years of pastoral ministry, I have found that wherever there is a breakdown in communication with a married couple, it can be traced to the absence of a mutually satisfying sexual relationship. The intimacy of a husband and wife's sexual relationship—its act of complete self-disclosure, mutual surrender and unselfish giving—is the heart of the marriage relationship.

Inverted sex does not contribute to the communication of a married couple. God made our bodies to relate to one another in sexual union in a way that is distinct from all the rest of creation: We're created to face one another. I don't want to seem tawdry in saying this, but a man has two hands that desire to touch a woman's two breasts. Lovemaking, kissing face-to-face and seeing each other eye-to-eye provide the far deeper possibility of expressing affection to *a person,* making it much more likely that a man and woman will truly be *together as one* than if they resort to the interplay of mouth-to-genitals stimulation. I propose that in the Creator's ingenious gift of our human capacity for sexual fulfillment, the soul-to-soul *visual and speech* capacities that communicate affection, devotion and fidelity are far and away the most profound and fulfilling aspects of sexual union—joined, of course, to the physical interaction of normal intercourse.

I am not espousing a prudish attitude toward lovemaking in marriage; that is, for example, I do not endorse the world's mocking stereotype that says only the "missionary position" is acceptable for Christians. I am, however, suggesting that beyond the evidence of the Scripture's challenge to resist the invasion of the world-spirit into our intimate lives, the dignity of the husband-wife relationship recommends face-to-face enjoyment of each other, as opposed to the dehumanizing practices of oral and anal sexual expression. This is not a commentary on faith but a question of personal ethics. Practices that depersonalize and debase do not strengthen marriages. In fact, the only reason people ask whether such practices are acceptable is because the Holy Spirit has put a check in their spirits.

Let me end with a caveat, however, because the Bible does not speak on this subject in conclusive words. I do not believe I am the final arbiter of what a loving married couple chooses for their own marriage love and play, and I do not reject someone who disagrees with my particular viewpoint. But I have learned from years of counseling couples that many are puzzled or are in disagreement regarding this, and others are weakened in their sexual desire for one another because a mate has become preoccupied with "tricks" rather than true intimacies. Thus, I have written this brief for a couple to discuss together—emphasizing that I never want to appear to preempt something they mutually have found meaningful. By that I mean that they have agreed on this form of lovemaking as an accepted part of their expression to one another, neither as a demand by one partner over the wishes and comfort level of the other nor as a substitute for normal sexual expression, but rather simply as foreplay.

Thus, for both single believers and married partners, I advocate that the Holy Spirit, not the world-spirit, define and sustain our values and practices in this regard.

SUGGESTED RESOURCES

BOOKS BY JACK HAYFORD FROM REGAL BOOKS

Available at www.regalbooks.com.

Blessing Your Children
Transmit a spiritual inheritance of substance and worth to the next generation by learning how to bless your children.

Fatal Attractions: Why Sex Sins Are Worse Than Others
Receive the biblical wisdom and real-world tools necessary to bring hope, healing and restoration from sexual violation in this companion to *The Anatomy of Seduction*.

Living the Spirit-Formed Life
Rediscover the power and blessings of such basic disciplines as prayer and fasting, daily worship and the release of repentance and forgiveness.

OTHER RESOURCES BY JACK HAYFORD

Available at www.jackhayford.org or by calling toll-free (800) 776-8180.

The Beauty of Spiritual Language: Unveiling the Mystery of Speaking in Tongues (Book)

Learn how speaking in tongues is neither gibberish nor emotional exuberance but is an intimate encounter with the heart of God.

Cleansed for the Master's Use (Audiocassette or VHS video)
Find a pathway of sanctification and deliverance in these three powerful teachings.

The Encyclopedia of Deliverance: Finding Freedom Through Christ and His Cross (24-audiocassette album)
Explore in depth an array of specific topics on spiritual warfare and liberation from bondage.

"Ex-Rated" Sex (4-audiocassette album)
Develop healthy attitudes about sex that are fundamental to a fulfilling marriage relationship.

The Holy Spirit: The Great Psychiatrist (2-audiocassette album)
Grow in a relationship with the Holy Spirit that invites discernment, wisdom and counsel into any situation of temptation or bondage.

Nehemiah: Pictures of the Holy Spirit (DVD)
Gain a deeper understanding of the book of Nehemiah in this video teaching from Jack Hayford's television broadcast, *Spirit Formed.*

Rebuilding the Real You: God's Pathway to Personal Restoration (Book)
Study the book of Nehemiah, which unfolds a clear picture of the nature and work of the Holy Spirit to assist the believer in rebuilding life's broken places.

INTERNET RESOURCES FOR EDUCATION AND SUPPORT

- Jack Hayford Ministries (www.jackhayford.org)
- The King's College and Seminary (www.kingsseminary.edu)
- Cleansing Stream Ministries (www.cleansingstream.org)

ENDNOTES

Chapter One

1. Jack W. Hayford, *Living the Spirit-Formed Life—Growing in the 10 Principles of Spirit-Filled Discipleship* (Ventura, CA: Regal Books, 2001), pp. 8-9. Used by permission.

Chapter Three

1. William A. Ogden, "He Is Able to Deliver Thee," 1887, public domain.

Chapter Four

1. *Oxford Dictionary*, compact ed., vol. 1 (New York: Oxford University Press, 1971), p. 1740.

Chapter Five

1. Gerhard Kittel, *Theological Dictionary of the New Testament*, vol. 4 (Grand Rapids, MI: William B. Eerdmans Publishing Company, 1967), p. 286.
2. Ibid.
3. The apostle Paul makes this distinction, saying, "I will pray with the spirit, and I will also pray with the understanding" (1 Cor. 14:15). He is in part discussing the broad subject of the use of Holy Spirit-enabled language in intercession, in worship, in prayer and in divinely aided adoration to the Lord. For more information, see appendix 5 of my book *The Beauty of Spiritual Language* (Nashville, TN: Thomas Nelson Publishers, 1996).

Appendix One

1. Jack Hayford, *I'll Hold You in Heaven* (Ventura, CA: Regal Books, 2003), pp. 38-39. Used by permission.
2. Ibid., pp. 39-40.

Appendix Three

1. With thanks to Pastor Chris Hayward, President, Cleansing Stream Ministries. Used by permission.

Appendix Four

1. "Let's Talk About Sex" from the show "Children Left Home Alone," *The Oprah Winfrey Show,* ABC-TV, January 14, 2004.

2. Kate Zernike, "Teenagers Want More Advice from Parents on Sex, Study Says," *The New York Times,* Dec. 16, 2003. http://www.teenpregnancy .org/about/announcements/news/pdf/NY%20Times%2012-16-03.pdf (accessed March 30, 2004).

3. "Let your marriage be held in honor in all things, and thus, let your marriage-bed be undefiled." K. S. Wuest, *The New Testament: An Expanded Translation* (Grand Rapids, MI: Eerdmans Publishing Company, 1961), p. 536.

    Lenski translates Hebrews 13:4 as "Honorable let marriage be in all respects, and the bed undefiled" and then comments, "The imperative is in place. Marriage is to be kept *HONORABLE*" (emphasis added). R. C. H. Lenski, *The Epistle to the Hebrews* (Minneapolis, MN: Augsburg Publishing House, 1966), p. 471.

    Word Biblical Commentary makes this observation: "The literary form [is] . . . set forth as direct imperatives . . . 'it must be respected' [that is, marriage]; 'it must be undefiled' [i.e., the marriage bed]." The gram-matical structure is formulated with the force of an imperative. William L. Lane, *Word Biblical Commentary,* vol. 47 (Dallas, TX: Word Books, 1991), n.p.